$\mathscr{A}$ MAGNIFICENT
BLUNDER

A MAGNIFICENT BLUNDER

From Divorce

and Despair

to Awe and Wonder

GARRY E. LEEP

XULON PRESS

Xulon Press
2301 Lucien Way #415
Maitland, FL 32751
407.339.4217
www.xulonpress.com

Unless otherwise indicated, Scripture quotations taken from the New King James Version (NKJV). Copyright © 1982 by Thomas Nelson, Inc. Used by permission. All rights reserved.

Printed in the United States of America.

ISBN-13: 978-1-54563-959-7

TABLE OF CONTENTS

INTRODUCTION

L ife is unpredictable. And with God, it seems like there's a surprise around every corner. Flipping through the Bible, you could get the idea that God wants to bless you. But getting a hold of those promises, or the God of those promises, often proves elusive. It had taken a long time, but life was good for me —solid-ground good. The prosperity cart of heaven (Psalm 65:11) had turned into a huge front-end loader that was dropping off bone-in cowboy rib-eye steaks at my home. It wasn't just dripping fat; it was dumping prime angus by the bucketload. Then suddenly, when I least expected it, life turned on a dime, and things got ugly—well, not so much ugly as really painful.

I suspect that the prophet Isaiah looked askance when the Lord commanded him to strip naked and prophesy for the better part of three years (Isaiah 20:2). Similarly, I had not entertained any desire to write this book and thus expose the three years of pain and nakedness of my soul. Ultimately, though, the God of all comfort reminded me of his purposes in bringing comfort to others (1 Corinthians 1:3-6). And so I sat down and wrote. I wrote of the gut-wrenching pain and the soul-rending despair. I wrote of the living nightmare of divorce and the subsequent journey into the dark night of the soul. Yet, if that were the only thing I had to offer here, I would be the first to pass on it. All of us have enough pain of our own, so no one needs an extra helping from me. But pain is the voice of God's love. Pain in any package can be the pathway that leads to an unbridled and boundless life!

Some will read this book and only see my pain; others will read and catch a glimpse of Jesus in my pain. My hope is that you will read these pages and be able to see Jesus in the midst of your pain, so that you can allow it to become a journey of awe and wonder.

CHAPTER 1
THE GOD WITHOUT LOVE

For God so loved the world that he gave his only begotten son, that whosoever believes in him shall not perish but have ever-lasting life.
—John 3:16

God is love, and he who abides in love abides in God, and God in him.
—1 John 4:16

Beloved, do not believe every spirit, but test the spirits, whether they are of God; because many false prophets have gone out into the world.
—1 John 4:1

Legend has it that the renowned twentieth-century Swiss theologian Karl Barth, when asked what was the most profound truth of the Bible that he had discovered after a lifetime of study, replied, "Jesus loves me, this I know, for the Bible tells me so." If this reality had informed the tenor of my childhood, the psychic and spiritual value would have been incalculable. But, alas, it was not to be. Instead, God, in his sovereignty, allowed for me to be the grandnephew of Barth's chief antagonist, Cornelius Van Til (and a grandson of Cornelius's oldest brother). During my boyhood days in the late 1950s and early 1960s, America

1

was still, in many ways, a country of European immigrants (all four of my grandparents were born in the Netherlands). Each ethnicity developed its own enclave when they reached American soil, and along with their possessions, they brought their language, culture, and religion. If you were Irish, it was presumed you were Catholic; if you were Dutch, you were likely Protestant — and of the Reformed persuasion.

America's God was the god who won World War II. The priest, the pastor, and the rabbi may have read from different sacred books, but the God they talked about had the same look. If you listened, you likely heard a similar message. They spoke of a "thou shalt not" God. In my upbringing, for example, there was no room for gray; everything was black and white. God was God, and everyone and everything else was not. This may have been good for God, but it wasn't for others. Authorities were always right, and children were to be seen, not heard. Adults in my orbit were mostly stoical, stern, and/or stubborn. Six days a week we spent in either Reformed day schools or churches. It was not a good environment for a sensitive and submissive soul.

In our Dutch Reformed homes, Bible reading followed hard upon supper each night, then polished off with prayer — all of this, I'm pretty sure, audible to me when I was still in the womb. There were variations, deviations, and endless permutations, but after all the biblical citations of violence and gore, hostile empires and war, the formula stood tall: people bad, God mad, people die. And if God wasn't mad, he just bored you to death. I was quick to accept the authenticity of this narrative because my own life read: Garry bad, authority mad, hell to pay! And even though one of my older sisters testified that I was easy to love as a child—and very well-behaved—fear, not love, was the coin of the realm.

As an adult, I came to realize that my mother's self-esteem had been built on God and her Dutch community's take on her parenting skills. The mantra of Dutch Reformed parenting was: "Spare the rod and spoil the child." Coupled with the old "one bad apple" axiom, this left my mother with little choice. She became Quick Draw McGraw with her hairbrush or wooden spoon on my bare behind. She was saving her children from a "Mom bad, God mad, we die" scenario. The physical pain was limited in scope and soon forgotten; it was the emotional pain that left lifelong scars. As my mother beat me with her ugly stick, *she* turned ugly—her face contorted in anger. Turning a dozen shades of red, she would scream, "Don't you ever sass me!"—her voice strained as if it were squeezing through the gates of hell, and the wooden spoon leaving a welt with each word. All in the name of a jealous, wrathful, vengeful, holy, get-even, sovereign God!

How did I get this god, whom one of my sisters once described as Grandpa Van Til with a hairbrush. Well, it wasn't from the Cornelius Brothers and Sister Rose; instead, it was from Grandpa Van Til and his brother Cornelius, my great-uncle Kees (pronounced "Case," the Dutch nickname for Cornelius). They certainly had their accomplices, most significantly throughout church history the likes of John Calvin and Augustine. And the Dutch Protestant churches as a whole took their doctrinal distinctives much more seriously in the mid-twentieth century than they do now. Today, the majority of pew-sitters in a Reformed environment might not even know what they believe on the destructive topic of *determinism*. On the other hand, I—with a world-renowned theologian/apologist for a great-uncle and his dueling eldest brother for a grandpa—had no say in the matter. These discussions are often more familiar in the halls of Protestant seminaries such as Westminster Seminary in suburban Philadelphia, of which Cornelius Van Til had been a cofounder and where he was a faculty member for many decades. In a legitimate defense of the complete work of Jesus on the cross, to save a broken and disoriented world, they came to differing conclusions as to how this all would be fleshed out. In their attempt to defend and free Christianity from religion's relentless effort to require humanity to work its way back to God, they developed a construct to support the Reformation's rallying cry of "faith alone in Christ alone."

Volumes have been written and endless debate has taken place—in polysyllabic words that are often understood only in the environs of theological studies—to describe God's logical sequence of thought as it relates to his sovereign will in determining who could spend eternity with him. The bottom line of these efforts is a God who only chooses a select minority for salvation in Jesus Christ; therefore, Jesus died for only the sins of this minority. As for the considerable majority, God has made no provision for their salvation, nor does he enlighten them about their need for salvation. And yet he holds them fully accountable for being sinners, hell being their just reward. And all this redounds to the glory of God!

CHAPTER 2
WHEN I LOOK BACK AT ALL THE CRAP I LEARNED IN HIGH SCHOOL ...

I call heaven and earth as witnesses today against you, that I have set before you, life and death, blessing and cursing, therefore choose life.
—Deuteronomy 30:19.

For this is good and acceptable in the sight of God our Savior, who desires all men to be saved and come to a knowledge of the truth. For there is one God and one mediator between God and men, the man, Christ Jesus, who gave himself a ransom for all.
—1 Timothy 2:3–6

The Lord is not slack concerning his promise, as some count slackness, but is longsuffering toward us, not willing that any should perish, but that all should come to repentance.
—2 Peter 3:9–10

Thank God, my parents were not mean by nature. I would have had a drinking problem by the time I was six! My dad was actually quite gentle and inclined to avoid conflict. My mother, undoubtedly incited by her upbringing and the pressures of church, Reformed theology, and our sequestered lifestyle, never embraced her eight children as God's wonderful gift to her—at least not past preschool age. When they grew up enough to show even the smallest propensity toward sin and to show evidence of their fallen nature, they became a burden that she bore from that day forward, and to different levels of distress before her God. They were God's, and she better act accordingly.

Before I was eight or nine, this background became the major contributor to my prominent thinking problem. By the time I was five or six, my mother had taught me a handful of card games. We started with "war," advanced to solitaire to keep me busy, and double solitaire when she had time to join in. Next came canasta, and I caught on quickly. On one occasion I held a killer hand and was readying my game-winning blow. Suddenly, from her perch near a kitchen window, my mother saw her father coming up our driveway in his two-tone olive-drab and light green Plymouth, with tail fins so tall they would make a shark envious. In great haste she said, "Give me your hand!" She had already gathered the take and discard piles, along with her hand. Distraught, I gave her my hand as if the cards represented a precious find on an archeological dig; I still did not have the slightest clue about what was going on. She hid the cards on a shelf underneath the table, where most families stored their Bible. (Our own Bible sat in a more prominent place, on top of the refrigerator, because we used it every night.)

My mother jumped up from her chair at the table and went to the door to greet Grandpa Van Til. I was getting my first sense of God entering the building. This left a new impression: it suggested that there were forces outside our home to hide from, namely Grandpa and God. Up until then, my worst fear was the thought of embarrassing my mother again as I had with my tears of separation anxiety near the end of the worship service in anticipation of her thrusting me into Sunday school. After Sunday school, I had returned home and retired to my room to change out of my Sunday finest. My mother opened the stairway door and yelled up to me that she would use the wooden spoon on my behind if I ever cried in church again. Now, introducing my grandpa into the mix, I was afraid that the wooden spoon might be growing some branches.

As I waited respectfully and impatiently for grandpa to leave, I brainstormed about how to sort out the cards and reconstruct the previous scenario. It had been a tight game, and I wanted to win; but suddenly I needed to know what Grandpa had a problem with. For various reasons, some Christians throughout the twentieth century had problems with cards, tobacco, dancing, movies, and alcohol. My grandpa's were more peculiar than most. Some saw cards as a threat to a household's well-being because the husband might gamble away his paycheck. My grandpa was supposedly concerned about their use in tarot readings. What I soon learned was that my grandpa saw problems with a lot of things, and he always made it God's problem, too.

A couple years later, I sat disconsolate at home one cool and crisp October evening. It was Halloween. When most of the boys my age were out soliciting candy from their neighbors, and some of the older boys might be igniting lunch bags of dog poop on a grumpy old man's stoop, I sat in the house with no hope of treating or tricking—as benign as that may seem. My evening was going to feature a visit by Grandpa and Grandma Van Til. That required that I get my homework done early so I could sit at attention, yet hoping never to draw the attention of the old and

7

stoical man we had come to think of as God in the flesh. That night I wouldn't be so lucky. While everyone else was likely chewing on Halloween candy, my grandpa beckoned me over to give me something else to chew on.

Not without his own indulgences, he pulled a shiny silver dollar from his pocket. As I stood next to his circular easy chair, he asked me if I knew the true meaning of this day in history. I was stumped. It wasn't Christmas, and it wasn't Easter—what could it be? I already knew that there never was a Santa Claus, and that there never was an Easter bunny. How was he going to suck the candy out of Halloween? I looked across the living room at my mother, knowing she hadn't taught me this one. She looked like she was hoping that telepathy might hold some powers in this awkward moment. But I couldn't pull an answer out of thin air. My grandpa rubbed the silver dollar and started throwing me hints, but I was working from a blank screen. Finally, he gave up hope and launched into a sermon on Martin Luther and the ninety-five theses he nailed to the church door. The silver dollar was still in view, and I was hoping for what I would identify in adulthood as a gracious ending. No such luck this time: Grandpa/God wrapped up his sermon and slid the coin back in his pocket. I looked at my mother for comfort, and she looked back at me with disappointment in her eyes. But I learned a couple quick lessons: God hates Catholics and God hates Halloween—and he was obviously none too fond of me for my ignorance.

My home environment kept me on alert. I soon learned that God could do and be things I wasn't allowed to be. Every Sunday I heard that he was a jealous God. This was the very sin that my mom used against me to try to get me saved when I was just a four-year old. She accused me of being jealous of my sister. I asked her why I couldn't simply live my life and be crucified at the end of it. A one-time crucifixion seemed a lot less painful than a lifetime of church and God. By the time I was nine, the tenets of Calvinism—as they were taught in my environment—were starting to overwhelm me. The first point of the Heidelberg Catechism should have brought great comfort to a Christian's soul. But my own thinking—that I belonged, body and soul, both in life and death, to my faithful Savior Jesus Christ—was cause for terror.

Living in an environment of being seen and not heard must have heightened the sensitivity of my eyes and ears. I had discovered that God didn't give two hoots for most people. I queried my mother as to which of her children she would have brought into existence just to send them to hell. She replied, "None, but I'm not God." Nonetheless, God was the one with superior discretion! All hope was lost, and I became afraid to die. I didn't want to go to hell, but I didn't have any interest in heaven either.

By high school, my religious training had reached critical mass. As juniors, we were being taught—by the only ordained minister on the teaching staff—the intricacies of the sovereignty of God and mankind's tainted freedom to choose. He regaled us with such references as God's "hardening Pharaoh's heart, loving Jacob but hating Esau, having the right as the potter to determine whatever he wanted to do with the clay," and so on. Exhausting both his list of Reformed arguments and the class with his lecture, he took a deep breath and launched into his coup de théâtre: "So, on one hand, God has sovereignly chosen whom he will save and whom he will not. On the other hand, man is held accountable for his eternal destiny. In order to accept this, one must give up the test of coherence. This is called faith!"

My whole soul shuddered. My teenage mind identified his statement as baloney. I did agree with him in his assessment that to believe such trash qualified as incoherence. At that moment I mentally dropped out, tacitly regarding myself as an atheist. Only decades later did I realize that I had been a seeker, and that the true God could no longer be sought in such an environment. I set out to fully enjoy what few days, weeks, or years I might have remaining to me this side of death.

CHAPTER 3

AND IT'S ONE, TWO, THREE–
WHAT ARE WE FIGHTING FOR?

*Vanity of vanities, says the preacher, vanity of vanities, all
is vanity.*
–Ecclesiastes 1:2

*For I know the thoughts that I think toward you, says the
Lord, thoughts of peace and not of evil, to give you a future
and a hope.*
–Jerimiah 29:11

My high school days were fast coming to an end. I
turned my energies toward after-school jobs and a
future college career. I wanted to set myself up to become
a millionaire and also to avoid the war that was still going
on at the time—way down yonder in Vietnam. The onset
of testosterone and the stupidity of other boys had begun
to erode my healthy perspective on women. Teenage girls,
with all their attendant insecurities, also made it evident that
they were no place to entrust your heart. Disqualified from
having a relationship with any "Christian girl," I opened
my eyes to other possibilities. But God, in his omniscience,
was looking out for me.

One late afternoon when I arrived at work, at the Royal
Crown Cola Company in East Chicago, Indiana, I started

chatting up a girl who lived right across the street from the bottling plant. She was pretty hot by a teenage boy's standards, and it looked like it might be easy to get her clothes off, since most of them were already missing. As our conversation picked up steam, an older cousin, who was a salesman for the soda-pop business, hopped out of his red Dodge convertible and beckoned me over. I had always admired Eddie: he was one of the older brothers of my best friend, Nick. He stood over six and a half feet tall, and I could well remember the night when, with his pretty fiancée next to him in his mint-green 1957 T-Bird, he unfolded his huge frame from his car to confront the fellow who had just crashed into it.

Now he was confronting me. In street language to get my attention, and with some level of disdain, he queried me as to my intentions. It was a significant moment. In his query he had—inadvertently or not—ascribed some manhood to me. He didn't preach a religious sermon to me; instead, he caused me to understand that he knew more about this girl than I did, and that I should have nothing to do with her. I turned from her and walked away, in reluctant repentance.

Changing jobs, I found myself in a new environment, with new challenges. One challenge was a mysterious teenage girl. I had no idea who she was, or where she had seen me, when I was paged on the intercom system at Strack and Van Til's, my cousin's grocery store. "Garry Leep in produce, answer the phone, please." I answered the phone and soon was listening to a girl I had never met but who was trying to convince me that I should go out with her. I was distressed, thinking I might be getting fired in the next few minutes for taking a personal phone call at work. I quickly gave her my home phone number and told her to call me before I left for work the next afternoon. The next afternoon arrived and, like clockwork, the phone rang at 3:45. It was the mystery girl. She began to sweet-talk me and entice me with her self-described physical attributes. In seeking to assure me that she was physically attractive, she suggested that it was no accident she was a majorette and a cheerleader at a local high school.

I had closeted myself as best I could in the back hallway of the kitchen, hoping my baritone voice would not reach my mother, who had been confined to her bedroom for the last six years with rheumatoid arthritis (and where she would spend 99 percent of the last thirty years of her life). Her arms or legs may have failed her, but her hearing was just fine. She heard whispers of my side of the conversation and wanted to know who I was talking to. I told her it was a girl, and from thirty feet, around three corners, and up a stairwell, she asked if the girl was from Illiana (the Christian high school in Lansing, Illinois, where I had been a student). I said no. And just as quickly as my teenage brain had allowed my imagination to run wild, the thrill was over. Mother told me to hang up the phone NOW! Her word was law and, much to my dismay, I never heard from the mystery girl again—or even discovered who she was. I was sure she would have taken me to places I had never seen before!

I soon embarked on my college career at Indiana University Northwest in Gary, Indiana, just five miles from our house. There they told me that I didn't need a college deferment from the military draft because I wasn't yet eighteen. Trusting my elders, I took one course under a full-time student load, which I would have needed to qualify for a deferment. This was partly because, at registration, my freshman status left me last in line, practically speaking, to get the classes and times I needed. As freshmen, we were finally allowed to enter a large auditorium on the second day of registration and "pull cards" for the classes we wanted to take—and at what times. It was only with the help of a senior, a friend from work (who had access to the cards at least a day before I did), that I was lucky enough to get twelve of the fifteen hours I needed on some kind of reasonable schedule, a schedule that would allow me to work almost full-time and attend college during daytime hours.

Since I turned eighteen by the time the semester ended, I went to get my deferment. But at the draft board they told me that I didn't qualify for a deferment because I would have needed three more credit hours in my first semester. I was now open to the luck of the lottery draft, something that would happen as soon as it could be determined whether a lottery for the draft was actually constitutional.

I continued to take required courses. And after some hapless efforts to find true romance, I sat down one day in an English comp class to discover that my unicorn was sitting right beside me. There, in all her glory, was a young woman I never knew could exist. Long raven hair, biblically blue eyes, slightly tanned and freckled porcelain white skin, Song of Solomon breasts—all decked out in a white blouse, a powder-blue miniskirt, with an intelligent and captivating smile. And she had that look for me! Rendered nearly speechless by the encounter, I set to work strategizing on how to *really* talk with her. The more my introverted and introspective personality worked on the problem, the more it became apparent that my soul was empty and that I had nothing to offer. Indicted by my own standards, I realized my need to grow up. Soon a draft notice from the army rescued me from that grim reality.

CHAPTER 4
I DON'T GIVE A DAMN, NEXT STOP IS VIETNAM

The pangs of death surrounded me and the floods of ungodliness made me afraid. The sorrows of Sheol surrounded me; the snares of death confronted me.
—Psalm 18:3-4

Then you will call upon me and go and pray to me, and I will listen to you. And you will seek me and find me when you search for me with all your heart. I will be found by you, says the Lord, and I will bring you back from your captivity.
—Jeremiah 29:12-14

Our soul has escaped as a bird from the snare of the fowlers; the snare is broken and we have escaped.
—Psalm 124:7

If anyone has a specific memory of September 5, 1972, it would likely be of the massacre at the Olympics in Munich, Germany, where numerous Israeli athletes were shot by the Palestinian terror group Black October. Before the next morning's news, eleven Israelis would be dead. My day didn't end that violently, though the nights preceding it were spent at liquor-fueled farewell parties that surely tested my guardian angels. On that Tuesday morning, the day after Labor Day, I hopped in the car, and my dad pointed it in the direction of the courthouse in Hammond, Indiana. I had never been outside the Dutch enclaves that lie around Chicago and Lake Michigan like a string of pearls for more than a week or two at most. That morning I was headed out to begin a two-year obligation in the US Army. My dad pulled up in front of the courthouse, and we exchanged a quick good-bye. As he drove away, I headed up the stairs to join the group of young men who were assembling for the bus ride to Chicago, and the subsequent flight out of O'Hare Airport.

No sooner had I engaged a young college grad named Dave in conversation, than he suddenly looked out at the street and exclaimed, "Oh My God, if they are drafting guys his age, this country is doomed." I turned around to see what he was talking about: there was my dad, in his nondescript gray work uniform, with his faux engineer's hat crowning his sixty-seven-year-old Fred Flintstone physique. He was just about to ascend the stairs to hand me the induction papers I had left on the car seat. I bent over in laughter and explained to Dave that it was my dad, and he was simply bringing me the papers and not joining us in the war effort. As it turned out, that was the most humor in uniform that I was going to experience.

The bus soon arrived and we headed to Chicago's AFEES (Armed Forces Examination and Entry Station), where one final check of our vitals was necessary to start the process of transforming us from civilians into government property. We soon took the oath to support the Constitution of the United States, and then we formed in long lines to receive our assignments. I begged the older African-American lady who was processing me not to send me to Fort Polk, Louisiana. I had already heard plenty of horror stories about that location, and anywhere else seemed preferable. Like a grandmother speaking to her grandson, she replied, "I'm sorry, son, but that's the only place I can send you today." Disappointment overwhelmed me for a bit, but after my first day of the "hurry up and wait" system that the armed forces are so good at, I was on a bus to O'Hare, where we joined more than 200 other draftees on a stretch DC-8 that was bound for England Air Force Base in Alexandria, Louisiana.

Army life was certainly an infringement on my freedom, but I hadn't come from a coddled background. If we weren't being trained for the dying days of America's involvement in the controversial quagmire of Vietnam, basic training would have mostly been an extended campout of guns, grenades, and rocket launchers, with a gas chamber thrown in for a challenge. The snakes, heat, and humidity were the biggest challenges for me while I served my time in the armpit of America, Fort Polk, Louisiana. During basic training, I had only one close encounter with a poisonous snake, and likewise with friendly fire, when a trainee got lazy in a live-fire exercise. When I moved on to combat-support training—in my case, cook school—I was soon surrounded with all the riffraff that the army could recruit in the first days of an all-volunteer military. One night I was roughly awakened by a fellow soldier, who looked me over and said, "I was just getting ready to kill you, but you're not the guy I was looking for." It's nice he wasn't a little drunker or crazier than he appeared to be.

Then, on a cold and gray Sunday morning in November, I watched with a contingent of fellow soldiers outside the barracks, as two others dragged a limp body off to the post hospital. Everyone figured Freddie was suffering from a Saturday night binge, but we soon found out differently. As a popular song of the time so succinctly put it, "Freddie's dead, that's what I said." So, too, was this our fellow soldier. A sleek stallion the day before, he was dead by late the next evening. It wasn't alcohol that killed him—it was meningitis. Back then no one knew very much about meningitis, but it was quick and it was deadly. Our barracks was immediately quarantined. All off-post passes were suspended, and we ate in the mess hall alone. Any of us who might have suggested an escape of the army post were met with the omnipresent threat of "twenty years to life" in the US Army's prison at Fort Leavenworth, Kansas, pounding big rocks into small ones. We were told it would make no sense going off to see a civilian doctor because they knew nothing about the disease. No point in getting a spinal tap to see if you had the bacteria; if you didn't have the bacteria, you could just as easily get it the next day and die in another two.

I was a mess. With the prospect of imminent death enveloping me like a rolling fog, I needed to find safe and sure solace from my Calvinistic misconceptions concerning the arbitrary and angry God of my childhood. As I searched high and low for what I needed, I stumbled on a chaplain's assistant, an ardent student of R. B. Thieme Jr., a pastor who had a biblical tape ministry headquartered in Houston. I was desperate, frantic to find answers to my questions. Thieme had answers—countless answers, it seemed. Thousands of hours of historical and doctrinal studies, along with verse-by-verse analyses of each book of the Bible, were available on tape from Thieme's Houston ministry.

Soon I heard the answer to what had become my most vexing question and the cause of my most frenzied searching. To paraphrase the Bible and Thieme: "God loved everyone (the Bible says "the world"), and Jesus died for the sins of the *whole* world (not just the elect). It would have been funny if it hadn't been so tragic. I was hearing the gospel—the good news!—for the first time. Twenty years of church had been bad news. Finally, I was hearing the *good* news, and for me it was great news! God was no longer an elitist, and he was no longer a bully. God was no longer just playing favorites, something I could never be. God was no longer in cahoots with the insiders. God was truly a loving, all-embracing Father. He had come to seek and to save those who were lost. Born into a spiritually dead environment, and schooled in biblical misconceptions for twenty years, I had been lost. But now I was found!

CHAPTER 5
IN THE DESERT WITH MISS GOLDEN HAIR

*And all the trees of the field shall know that I the Lord have
brought down the high tree and exalted the low tree, dried up
the green tree and made the dry tree flourish.*
—Ezekiel 17:24

*He turns the wilderness into pools of water and dry lands into
watersprings. When they are diminished and brought low,
through oppression, affliction and sorrow, he pours contempt
on princes and causes them to wander in the wilderness where
there is no way. Yet he sets the poor on high, far from affliction.
Whoever is wise will observe these things, and they will understand the lovingkindness of the Lord.*
—Psalm 107:35, 39, 40, 41a, 43

The search for the God and father of Jesus, instead of the
god of my forefathers, took four months. I had gone
through cook school and had been posted as "permanent
party" at the base hospital as a mess cook. My soul was
raw and worn. But as the multitude of tapes from Houston
rolled for two hours every day and for eight to ten hours on
my days off, my life changed. I was ecstatic. The goodness
of God was unfathomable.

My nondescript active service continued for a little more than another year. I took a three-month "early out" to avoid another summer at Fort Puke, Lousy-anna, opting instead for a year of active reserves, which only required monthly meetings and a two-week summer camp. I soon went to live with my oldest brother and his family, helping him in his newly acquired pizza shop in Hopkins, Minnesota, as I considered my options in either going to work or returning to school. All the while, the truths of the Bible continued to give my life a form of purpose and meaning that I had never known before.

My time with my big brother soon ended. After eight short weeks of staying with him, the Lord called him home when he was only thirty-nine years old. Left with a restaurant to run, I quickly made pizza sauce and Italian sausage my focus—without any recipes to guide me. I had watched my brother make them, and with him it had been all eyeball measurements. I then built and baked pizza after pizza for friends and family to see how close I could come to replicating his masterpieces. But the loss of my brother and the long hours took their toll. I was a trim and fit twenty-two-year-old, but one morning, as I waited to pay for my order at a purveyor's office, I had to grab the counter to keep from falling down in fatigue. I realized that it was time to make plans to sell the shop and return to school.

Within six months, I had sold the shop for 150 percent of my brother's purchase price, and I was enrolled at Grace College in Winona Lake, Indiana. Eager to engage in preparation that might bolster the spiritual gift of a pastor-teacher, I signed up for two summer sessions of biblical Greek. What was I thinking! It turned out that the courses, which were offered to incoming and present seminary students, represented a quick review of the semesters of Greek they had already taken. On the other side of the spectrum was me: I had only reluctantly taken Spanish in high school and had retained nothing of consequence. There I was, covering two new chapters a day, thirty new vocabulary words, numerous noun declensions and verb conjugations. In the ninety-degree heat of my campus apartment, I sat in the bathtub for hours with my Greek book in hand and my skin turning prunelike, as I kept the water cool and surrounding me.

After a year of successful academics, which nonetheless left me broke, I went down to central Indiana for the summer. Joe, my friend from Grace College, had arranged a job for me and a place to stay. In what felt like another life—in which I was separated from and ostracized by my family and previous friends for my new religious views—I began attending a small doctrinal church. Thieme, though he had a tape ministry, had often said, 'If you find a local church teaching Bible doctrine, shut off your tape recorder and go." So I did.

At first, all seemed fine. The local pastor's teaching was similar to what I had heard on the Houston tapes. But as I listened for a while, it seemed that his teaching was a little *too* similar—identical, in fact—to Thieme's messages. This concerned me some. I expected a pastor to put himself before the Bible and the Lord, not just a tape recorder, to prepare for his sermons. When I queried others in the church, no one seemed to have an issue with this. Dumb me! What was I thinking?

I dismissed my concerns and soon found myself distracted from any further considerations of the subject by a pretty young woman. I had caught sight of her on an earlier visit to the church with Joe, but now both she and I were there full-time. Could I really be this lucky? Was this God's "right woman" for me? I was certainly hoping so!

Right woman. Right woman? RIGHT WOMAN! This was quite the concept. It was taught to us as biblical truth. Thieme's doctrine was developed around God's provision for Adam in the form of Eve. It was likely preached to tens of thousands of young singles throughout the United States and around the world. At first blush, the teaching sounded so right; but ultimately, like all biblical distortions, it proved to be destructive in so many ways. Thieme enunciated the notion that God had only one right mate for every person. Further, if one remained in God's plan, which mostly revolved around a positive attitude toward Bible doctrine, then one could expect marriage to be phenomenal. Tell this to a testosterone-driven young man, and his sexual imagination could fill up the first twenty years of marriage. He would be marrying a goddess! By the same token, a single woman's imagination could read into the script whatever her heart desired. Move over, Prince Charming, here comes my Right Man!

But, instead of enjoying the pursuit of a young woman with a relaxed mind and an open heart, the necessity of identifying someone as your right mate turned what should have been fun and playful into a religious chore. Furthermore, living in the fishbowl of a forty-member local church meant that everyone was aware of everyone else's business. And Dick Jones, the pastor of this church, was the biggest snoop of all.

My initial efforts to date Annie fell flat. We were both introverted, insecure, and fearful of failure in the fishbowl. Any real initiative that I offered, she rebuffed. I was confused. This was the only "sanctioned" church within sixty miles; altogether, there were only three eligible women, and the other two did nothing for me. So it was either Annie or no one. I was despondent. The years came and went with no other church-sanctioned options. No one really joined our church from the outside, and what amounted to five or six dates over four or five years went nowhere. In the interim, my friend Joe brought his Marine aviator buddy to town and introduced him to Annie. It looked like a real match from my vantage point. I guess God didn't have a spouse designed for me. My time and opportunity had run out.

But Annie and the Marine didn't last. The excitement of dating the radar intercept officer was short-lived, and just before the church's first wedding—in which Joe married *his* "right woman"—the touted couple broke up, and it turned out that Annie was the one who broke it off. That happened on a Friday night, and by Sunday morning Annie was hearing from the pulpit that, if she kept rejecting her "right man" candidates, she would eventually go into "reversionism," which was Pastor Jones's term for developing a bad attitude toward the pastor and his message, and that would, in turn, culminate in dying the "sin unto death," God's ultimate discipline. This was fear-mongering at its worse, but it was very effective.

Apparently, this declaration on Pastor Jones's part scared Annie into giving me a second look, and in due time she made it obvious that she was interested in me. I was unaware of the underlying fear that rekindled her interest, but I took full advantage of my opportunity—an opportunity that produced a marriage that was dead on arrival. Two sensitive souls we were, and we were joined in holy matrimony after being tyrannized for ten years in this doctrinal cult, which had bruised and battered our souls. The cult had robbed us of everything: we married, but our hopes and dreams became a living nightmare.

As I look back on those dark and dreadful days, words cannot really begin to convey the scope of my hopelessness. For ten years I had invested all I could of myself in this cult movement that was mislabeled a church. My personhood had consolidated itself around the only thing left to cling to. The church had robbed me of all my dreams except the hope of a happy marriage. In the process of obedience to "Bible doctrine," I had gutted my soul. Now the marriage had arrived and was dead. Nothing I could say or do would work. Like the poor couple in the song Sister Golden Hair, Annie and I couldn't meet anywhere near the middle, nor in the air. It was hard to love just a little. We were definitely in the desert on a horse with no name, but considering the road we were on, I would have dubbed him Good Intentions. I was trapped, and there was no way out.

CHAPTER 6
FLOCK ABUSE

"This is what the Sovereign Lord says: Woe to the shepherds of Israel who only take care of themselves! Should not shepherds take care of the flock? You eat the curds, clothe yourselves with the wool and slaughter the choice animals, but you do not take care of the flock. You have not strengthened the weak or healed the sick or bound up the injured. You have not brought back the strays or searched for the lost. You have ruled them harshly and brutally.
—Ezekiel 34:1–4.

Apparently, Pastor Jones had spent his wedding night at his mother-in-law's house in a bedroom next to hers. That's special—so special that Annie and I paid a terrible price some fifteen to twenty years later. Our whole wedding plan had to be approved by him. He said that someone had to be the authority of the wedding, and since he was officiating at the ceremony, he would naturally be that someone.

Annie had hoped her sisters would be her bridesmaids. She had asked them, and they all happily accepted. When Jones heard this at his weekly meeting with me (Annie was not allowed to join us in these discussions about marriage), he nixed the whole idea. The sisters' husbands or boyfriends didn't go to our church, and one had long hair and a beard. If they were to be in any of the wedding pictures, it would desecrate the wedding. Instead, it devastated Annie.

On a parallel front, Jones said that God no longer loved us, and we were too dumb to talk to him. This was not an overnight development. One of the methods of a developing cult is to abuse the truth by means of the increasing use of centralized authority. Eventually, the frog finds himself boiled, never realizing that the water (truth) is getting hotter (authority). Thieme, the Houston tape pastor, had an undergraduate emphasis in history and Greek. He then attended Dallas Theological Seminary and graduated with top honors. He had the privilege of being taught by none other than Lewis Sperry Chafer, the founder of the seminary. Chafer's *Systematic Theology,* published close to a century ago, is still highly regarded and frequently used in evangelical circles. Chafer's theology and the seminary's academic training were the foundation of Thieme's teachings, and it was a great foundation. We were well taught in the basic Bible doctrines pertaining to salvation. We knew that our salvation was paid for in full by Jesus Christ, that we were eternally secure, and that we had a remarkable future in front of us, one that would soon start in time and continue forever in eternity. If our souls were not being fed, our intellect certainly was. In Thieme's teaching we had a wealth of information that gave us confidence before both God and men.

But somehow the wheels began to come off, or, as we had been taught concerning the fate of others, we were drifting off course from grace. We were told that "drifting" from grace was a nautical term indicating that a ship had gotten a little off course; over the expanse of a large body of water, the ship would end up way off course. A mixture of 99 percent truth and 1 percent falsehood will do this: the truth keeps you glued to your seats until it is too late.

Part of the 1 percent was attitude. The whole doctrinal cult was built on the misunderstanding that good military leadership translates into good church leadership. Thieme had had a stateside military career that roughly paralleled the duration of World War II. It seemed that the cult functioned as if we were new trainees who had just been introduced to the rigors of military life. In the military, this generally lasted during boot camp and possibly during some advanced training. In the cult, we were belittled and talked down to for twenty years. The leadership became increasingly destructive, at least to the souls of those who were obedient followers of what was spoken from the pulpit.

Thieme was in many ways an impressive personality. He came from a proud family background, was intelligent, had a successful military career, and graduated from a highly regarded seminary with honors. He was an interesting, even entertaining speaker, and he had established a pulpit ministry to thousands; furthermore, he carried himself with class and a sense of humor. By contrast, Jones was a sycophant and a wannabe. The youngest brother of a bunch of World War II Marine veterans, he was disqualified from military service because of flat feet. If one were to summarize his person, flat would be an apt description. He was unable to relate to anyone he couldn't exert his position over; in later years he would actually turn and run from any casual street encounter with someone who had left his church. Although he had matriculated at a well-regarded college and seminary, he soon replaced any genuine study with simply parroting back to us what he had heard on tapes from Houston.

I later discovered that Jones had developed the skill of cutting his own hair with electric clippers. He probably was well suited to barbering: he could have listened in on all the juicy gossip in a barbershop or salon, and it would have only taken someone's hair two to three months to recover from one of his hack jobs. Recovering from his hack job on our souls took more than a decade.

It began to look as though Thieme was impressed with his own intelligence and academic skills, because he was beginning to use these to develop new doctrines. Some of his discoveries were truly a blessing; but as time went on, they became less faith-based and relationally based—less and less about Jesus or Bible doctrine, and more and more about intricate formulas that were missing the point. Eventually, they stepped over the line into false teachings of great consequence. One of the greatest errors was Thieme's announcement, parroted by Jones, that God could not love us. We were sinners, and God cannot have anything to do with sin. God could only love the righteousness of Christ that had been imputed to our souls at the time of salvation. Therefore, our point of contact with God became his justice. The use of the word "love" in the American vocabulary was weak and wimpy, he said, and something had to be done. God could not be party to weakness. Problem solved: God was now a God of integrity, and that was far superior to love anyway. Furthermore, if a person had not attained the status of spiritual maturity, it made no sense for her to pray. Any of us who would have suggested we were spiritually mature would have been expressing the height of arrogance. We were told to simply confess our sins to God and leave real prayer to someone mature enough to know what he was doing—like the pastor!

For the previous ten years we had met to listen to Bible doctrine for six hours a week. Our church services consisted of an opening prayer, an hour of teaching, and a closing prayer. That happened twice on Sunday morning, Sunday night, Wednesday night, Thursday night, and Friday night. The hour of teaching included word-for-word exegesis of the biblical text from the original languages. Extensive doctrines were developed around that exegesis. We might write down twenty detailed points on a topic, only to have it revised two weeks later, when we were expected to rewrite it once again. Teachers might argue that repetition is good. But spending five solid years in the book of Romans alone, and about seven years exclusively in the book of Hebrews, might be considered a little over the top.

These academic methods were then used to diminish any believer who hadn't learned under similar constraints. All other believers became suspect. We were gradually influenced to give up any meaningful relationships with those outside the group. These inferior believers were ignorant at best and evil at worse. Interesting history tales were told to promote a right-wing mindset more intensive than the Red Scare. Although much of what was said had some truth to it, it wasn't used to develop a love relationship with God, others, our enemies, or ourselves. Like so many Protestants have done to varying degrees, we made the Bible into an idol, as opposed to developing a love relationship with Jesus. And God forbade us ever to utter the name "Jesus" without saying "The Lord Jesus Christ." None of this lovey-dovey, Jesus-freak stuff! Jesus is God of the armies, not some longhaired wimp.

Our souls were sacrificed on the altar of Bible doctrine. We had been repeatedly taught that, as sheep, we were too dumb to read the Bible to any personal benefit. In the meantime, the pastors (shepherds) were using the word of God to oppress us. To survive our increasing pain, we had to transmit that oppressiveness to others. We became mean, petty, cruel, legalistic, chauvinistic, and myopic.

Ultimately, we bore the brunt of the oppression: in some form or another, we were self-haters.

The God from ten years before was long gone. The joy of my salvation had disappeared. How could this have happened? For ten years I had sat down, shut up, and listened. I had given up my dreams to support a church, but that disintegrated into a platform for a tyrant. Now I found myself isolated and abandoned, with no place to turn for even a little commonsense counseling. Jones had said he did not have the spiritual gift of counseling. He told us that no one in our group did either. Soliciting advice outside the group, be it from friends, family, or professionals, would put us on the road to the "sin unto death," for their advice could only be evil.

Annie was a quiet and private person. There was hardly a place that was private enough, either physically or psychologically, for us to have a meaningful conversation during our courtship. She had intimated that, when we were married, that would change. I figured that we knew each other: we had listened to the same teaching for ten years and had shown unwavering devotion to it; therefore, we must be on the same page. We married too quickly, for if we had waited, we would not have married at all. The cult had destroyed any freedom to live and love. I had messed up and married someone else's "right woman." God was really mad at me. What was I going to do?

For days, weeks—even months—I walked around in fear and trembling. As a child, punishment had always been swift and sure. My mother's hairbrush or wooden spoon on my bare behind came quickly after the slightest ungodly infraction. In adulthood I expected no less from God. How was the sin-unto-death going to happen? Death never came! After a while I quit cowering. There were occasions as a child when my infraction so infuriated my mother that, fearing an anger-driven punishment, I would run from her. Doing so would intensify the threat of "just wait until your father gets home." That was a long and terrible wait. Sometimes my father would punish me; but more often he wouldn't. Months were passing here in my adulthood, and for whatever reason, I wasn't getting disciplined. Maybe God just wasn't in the mood to kill me.

Little did I know that the Lord was busy on my behalf. He was very likely quite mad by this time—just not at me. In Ezekiel 34, the text I referred to earlier, God has many expectations of shepherds, or those who take responsibility for his people. Jesus speaks of himself as the Good Shepherd in John 10:14–15. He declares that he lays down his life for his sheep. And he expects no less from those who would call themselves pastors, or under-shepherds.

Jones had squeezed us for every dime he could get. Although he was by no means getting rich, he was becoming more and more domineering. As we showed increasing commitment to the church, he used our loyalty to infiltrate every aspect of our lives. Though he was a weak and wimpy person off the pulpit, his pulpit personality was loud, mean, and dogmatic. He behaved as though he were the last line of defense in a high-security prison. He had none of the characteristics of a shepherd: that is, he showed no consideration, no compassion, no healing technique, and no concern for us personally. We were simply cannon fodder for his misguided notion that he had the spiritual gift of pastor-teacher. He was a false teacher who displayed none of the fruits of the Holy Spirit of God. He was a control freak who was under pressure, ready to explode before our very eyes.

The woe God promised this pastor if he did not change was to come later—years later. For the time being, God was behaving toward him in a way that so beautifully depicts God: as "a gracious and merciful God, slow to anger and abundant in lovingkindness, one who relents in doing harm" (Jonah 4:2). In the meantime, God was coming to my rescue—only not in a way that I expected.

CHAPTER 7
THE GENIUS SHEPHERD

*For thus says the Lord God: "Indeed I myself will search for
my sheep and seek them out. As a shepherd seeks out his flock
on the day he is among his scattered sheep, so will I seek out
my sheep and deliver them from all the places where they were
scattered on a cloudy and dark day."*
—Ezekiel 34:11–12

*"I will feed my flock, and I will make them lie down," says the
Lord God. "I will seek what was lost and bring back what
was driven away, bind up the broken and strengthen what
was sick."*
—Ezekiel 34:15–16.

God is a genius. Where someone else might have come
along and tried to move me out of the cult in order
to heal me, the Great Shepherd came to his sheep. There
he began to use circumstances to effect my healing. Our
greatest wounds are often self-inflicted, and we are frequently oblivious to our own destruction. We hear things
from pulpits that are self-proclaimed to be the voice of God;
instead, they are words used by men with their own demons,
their own agendas, and their own pain. In an effort to apply
these words to myself, I found that they were destructive;
and when I applied them to my marriage, the destruction
became apparent.

As time went by, and my marital failures mounted, there seemed to be few alternatives left. Not divorce, not suicide— but maybe, just maybe, I could get away with a prayer. I had grown up in a "Christian family" where prayer was rote. There was the one I recited as a small child in which I was reminded every night that I might die before I woke up. Then there was the standard prayer my father uttered slowly and wearily at the supper table every night after another boring chapter of the Bible had been read. As a rambunctious child and an intense teenager, these prayer models hadn't left a positive impression on me. As I have said earlier, the cult had dissuaded us of any notion we might have had that we were capable of any meaningful conversation with God. Instead, we had turned our lives over to sin confession and using formulas and problem-solving devices that had become more psychological, less biblical, and not at all relational.

In a feeble attempt to find help in the midst of my confusion, I crept to my prayer closet (bedroom), closed the door, got down on my knees, and asked God to show me how to love my wife. I have to smile as I think back to that prayer, in terms of my present perception of God. A loving God had shepherded me to a point where I would speak to him. As a proud father holds his infant child in his arms, trying to coax the first words from his mouth, so God had led me to where I could finally speak. And what did the proud Shepherd hear? Baaa, baaa, baaah! He had broken the ice in our long-cold relationship. After thirty years, I had allowed myself to say something meaningful to God, and I asked him for his help.

Soon I began to experience his help. Asking God for aid took some of my burdens off me and put them on him. Instead of my problems as the center of my universe, God had become that center. Even though we had been robbed of a loving God, we still had an honorable and honest God whom we could expect to treat us fairly. If he chose to be gracious and merciful instead of disciplining us, we could count ourselves lucky. Furthermore, conversation with a *person* fosters relationship. I was turning from applying some faith-rest concept or other technique to a *person*. Many have assumed that the Bible and God are the same. We have often become well acquainted with the Bible without ever making God's acquaintance. Such was my dilemma.

What little relationship I had with God began to diminish the pastor's authority in my life to some degree. I could, in turn, start looking at Annie relationally, instead of trying to keep her doctrinally in line. We had been taught that marriage was a state of authority, not love, and it was a wife's responsibility to submit to her husband's authority. Years later we learned that Jones had entertained the idea of having Annie stand up in front of the congregation during our courtship and chastise her for not being submissive and responsive with regard to the wedding plans. This was no idle threat. A few years before that, my college friend Joe and I had been ordered to stand up in front of the church and were told we had five minutes to forget some notions we had acquired or leave the church. We decided to leave; but later that Sunday afternoon, we decided that we had no real place to go, so we returned to face our public discipline. I suspect Amish shunning would look good by comparison. As I directed what love I could toward Annie, I began to see things again in her that I could enjoy. Slowly, as I tried to mitigate the abusiveness coming from the pulpit, which I was supposed to direct toward Annie, I also decided God didn't expect me to treat myself any worse than I treated her. It was a small start. Growing up, we had often heard the command to "love your neighbor as yourself." It had never occurred to me, when I heard that, that you had to love yourself in order to love your neighbor as yourself. I don't think it had occurred to the adults who surrounded me either. Their manner of life did not suggest that they felt much love. There was no viable value to my person as a child. If there were to be any, it would be conditional, and I would have to create it and earn it.

Now, as a husband, I had a neighbor (wife) who, if left unloved, was going to cause me to self-destruct. As I tried to cut Annie as much slack as possible, I decided that perhaps I should start cutting myself some slack as well. In my first twenty years, I had heard that I was totally depraved; and for the next ten years, I was taught that I was no damn good. Now God was using a helpmate to help me see that I, too, was loved. Slowly, despite the pastor's efforts to the contrary, our relationship stabilized, and there was some hope, even though I had married the "wrong woman." We were told that, despite the fact that we had both married the wrong person, "if we lived life with integrity, it could be livable."

Concurrent with these kindnesses, God also used the cruelties of man and circumstance to our advantage. On our wedding day, before we left on our honeymoon, we stopped at my apartment. My new bride removed her contact lenses, and in the process, closed the bathroom sink drain to ensure that she wouldn't lose them. As it turned out, one of the faucets had a slow drip. Annie forgot to unplug the drain before we left the apartment, and over the course of a few hours the sink overflowed and continued to overflow in our absence. When we returned two weeks later, the landlord gave me an eviction notice. The water coming down from my apartment had caused a great portion of the downstairs ceiling to fall to the floor. There was considerable damage. Both the landlord and his son had been my close friends and fellow members of the cult. His son soon returned to being our friend, but by that time we had been thrown out of the duplex, the other half of which was occupied by "our church" (Jones had his study in an upstairs bedroom).

Subsequent to this, my job in IT at one of the local banks was outsourced, along with the whole department. For the previous five years I had worked at the bank under a fellow cult member, who had been transformed from a fairly reasonable person into a chauvinistic fanatic who had started writing letters to the editor of the local newspaper that made his employer cringe. My friend Don, the church's lone deacon, highly offended by my boss's offensive articles, went to Jones and questioned him about how he could endorse such public nonsense by being such a close friend of my boss. Interestingly, when he was confronted, Jones backpedaled. Nonetheless, Don felt he was running the risk of confronting God and looking "the sin unto death" in the eye. Don was the pastor's senior by a dozen years in age and light years in life, yet the water was boiling him alive, too. Though I was thrust into unemployment, which proved difficult, it freed me from on-the-job cultic oppression. What a relief to be done with that boss!

My unemployment set in motion a move out of the small city where Annie and I were living into the countryside in order to find more affordable housing. Since she and I had both been raised in rural settings, it returned us to a more relaxed environment. Our mental health soon benefited from planting a garden and raising some dogs. Not long after that, Annie's longtime job at the other local bank disappeared. We now were both without real jobs, and we never considered collecting unemployment: that would have been engaging in the evils of socialism. We began to lose weight due to the fact we could not afford adequate food and our garden did not produce enough to feed two adults. Although it was an effective weight-loss program, I don't recommend it! Temporary work and selling blood plasma became part of our lives. No one in church ever offered any help, perhaps because we had been taught to allow other people to have their privacy. We had also been taught how noble the self-sufficiency of the early pioneers in the western United States had been. They were so noble that they would die before they would go to their neighbor for food in the middle of a winter blizzard.

But God was smiling on us. Adversity made us focus on our immediate problems and made us more of a team. It also required that I leave town for truck-driving school in order to find some full-time—if only temporary—work. It was a blessing for me to be removed from the church by my over-the-road assignments, driving a moving van from coast to coast for the summer. I was unable to be in church or listen to the six hours of weekly teaching that continued in a machine-gun staccato aimed at our souls. The summer driving job ended, and it was back to church, temporary jobs, and selling blood plasma. Nevertheless, the interruption had a positive effect, and soon I was moving in the direction of a permanent full-time job. The new job fit better than anything I had done since my teens and contributed to a happier environment for both of us.

Then, one Sunday morning, a real God-thing happened! As I waited for Annie to finish up in the bathroom before we headed for church, I turned on the television. Typically, there was nothing of interest on at that time of the week. But as I absently flipped through the few broadcast channels we received, I came upon a pastor from Atlanta whose name was Charles Stanley and whose television show was called *In Touch*. We had been taught to deride anyone who did not teach the Bible in a word-for-word, verse-by-verse method. But as I sharpened my attention in order to find something to be critical of, I couldn't see anything that was amiss. I thought to myself, "I wonder what Jones would find wrong with this." I soon turned off the TV, and we headed for church. But the next Sunday morning I returned to that television channel, and, thank God, so had Charles Stanley. As I listened intently, I felt a relief coming to my soul. I found nothing he said that did not line up doctrinally with what we had been taught. He may not have taught exegetically from his pulpit, but his doctrinal content was nothing Jones could have condemned.

After overcoming that obstacle, it was no longer what Dr. Stanley said that was my focal point, but rather the way he said it. Except for a brief interlude as a nine-year-old, when our pastor was kind enough to visit me when I was in the hospital with a broken arm—and the initial joy as a twenty-year-old when I heard that God loved everybody— my soul had been ravaged in the name of God for most of my thirty-seven years. Now something different was going on. Charles Stanley's demeanor was so kind, so gentle, and so compassionate that I thought, if God were anything like Charles Stanley, things would be okay. Listening to Charles Stanley on a frequent basis got my wheels of thought into further motion: I began to converse with a trusted friend more about God and less about Bible doctrine, and I began reading Christian books again. We had been told that we were better off with one bad authority (speaking with one voice) than two good ones (presumably with competing messages). This supposed rationale from a genius like

Napoleon was the reason we were no longer allowed to read other Christian literature, even books published by Thieme.

My thoughts returned to the days I spent in northern Indiana attending a different doctrinal church while I was attending Grace College. The pastor, Bill, was friendly and outgoing. He was relaxed in the pulpit, he patiently entertained my questions, and he even invited me to Sunday dinner with his family. Now, after my time in the cult, I privately wondered whether even Bill had morphed into an angry tyrant from the pulpit.

By this time, I was the sales manager of a small sandwich company with an extensive territory to cover. One morning I decided to work my way as far north in my territory as possible. Late in the afternoon, I skipped up to Fort Wayne to see if I could locate Bill. In God's providence, I was able to find the church's new location, and to my great delight, Bill was in his study. Bill remembered me from more than fifteen years before, and he caught me up on what had transpired in his life and ministry. Instead of becoming narrower and more controlling, he had blossomed into a pastor equipped by God to deal with the changing cultural landscape in a kind and loving way. After a three-hour visit, I hurried the hundred-plus miles home to tell Annie what had transpired. As I bounded into the house in excitement, my intense personality could hardly be contained. And Annie was more than a bit curious when I filled her in on my visit with Bill.

In our doctrinal cult, the pressures from the pulpit were reason not to trust your intimate thoughts to anyone. Unless your relationship with a spouse or friend preceded your relationship with the church, the likelihood was that sooner or later your thoughts would end up getting to the pastor, especially if they could be construed as dangerous to the group in any way. Though Annie and I had met in the cult, she was trustworthy; but I didn't want to burden her with my nonconformity. We held many things close to our vest, never really sharing our innermost thoughts. As an example, I had decided not to have children because I did not want to expose them to the church. If we couldn't get out, the least we could do would be not to bring children in. Annie had concluded the same, except that her decision was based more on the difficulties of our relationship.

Though Annie was curious about Bill's church, she met my exuberance with her typical reticence. But she was interested enough that we planned a trip north to attend the church. It wasn't very long before we were able to escape our church for an evening, and to travel up to Fort Wayne for a weeknight service. We were more than a little surprised by the feel in that church. Despite the fact that Bill engaged in the same exegetical style of teaching that we were accustomed to and had come to expect, the vibe in the room and from those in attendance was remarkably different. There was interaction between Bill and his listeners. There was a relaxed demeanor and a pleasant interaction among the congregation. There wasn't the oppressiveness that comes from an atmosphere of fear-mongering and anxiety.

After the service, we spent some time with Bill, and then on our way home we stopped at a pleasant restaurant to celebrate the evening with an excellent steak dinner. As we sat across from each other with an adult beverage in hand, we reveled in what had to have been the best night of our marriage up to that point! It was an evening served up by a gracious and loving God, whether grace had been said over it or not. As the Old Testament says, God was "causing his face to shine upon us." We anxiously looked forward to him smiling on us again.

CHAPTER 8
I FEEL THE EARTH MOVE
UNDER MY FEET

In my distress, I called upon the Lord, and he heard my voice
from his temple.
—Psalm 18:6

Then the earth shook and trembled, the foundations of the hills
also quaked and were shaken, because he was angry.
—Psalm 18:7

The Lord thundered from heaven.
—Psalm 18:13

The foundation of the world was uncovered.
—Psalm 18:15

He delivered me from my strong enemy, from those who hated
me, for they were too strong for me.
—Psalm 18:17

As I continued to listen to Charles Stanley, my heart began to soften, and thoughts from bygone years began to resurface. One morning Annie and I had occasion to stop and visit a friend at her women's clothing shop. After Annie had perused the season's offerings, the three of us stood around talking among the latest fashions. Annie, our friend, and I must have somehow been sharing the same lament. We'd been promised if we assimilated Bible doctrine in our souls, it would eventuate in knowing God. Out of nowhere, some words came tumbling out of my mouth.

"You know, we've been listening to Bible doctrine for twenty years. When are we going to know Jesus?"

I recalled lying in bed early one Saturday morning when I was a teenager, and my four-legged dresser started to walk across the floor. It was an earthquake that was rattling everything in my bedroom. Here in our friend's dress shop, I didn't feel any vibrations, but I should have. God had placed the words in my mouth, and I had spoken! It wasn't long before the earth moved under our feet and the sky came tumbling down. The Shepherd had healed me enough so that he could move me. He was coming to our rescue—and was definitely shaking things up!

The changes now came fast and furious. My friend Joe was in the Marine Reserves and still chomping at the bit to see some wartime action. When Saddam Hussein invaded Kuwait to set the stage for the Gulf War, it also set the stage for Joe to pull his family out of our church, because he soon embarked on active duty and was stationed a thousand miles away. Separated from church, Joe's first instinct was to start listening to tapes from Thieme. Somehow, in the process, he stumbled on two pastors who had been part of Thieme's inner circle. These men, unlike Jones, had continued to study the Bible and in doing so were discovering a refreshing and dynamic view of God.

Joe soon talked about these pastors with his mother-in-law, who had been instrumental in maintaining the financial stability of our cult. In no time, she was listening to one of those pastors and quickly paid a visit to his church in Dallas. A few more months passed, and during that time she sold her two businesses and made plans to move south to be a part of the Dallas church that she had been attending sporadically. In spite of her efforts to leave Jones's "church" as quietly as she could, there was no such possibility in the cult. When Jones caught wind of her plans—and thought she had made her final appearance—he castigated her from the pulpit for fifteen or twenty minutes before he even began the Bible teaching. He made every negative comment he could possibly make about her, including the suggestion that she probably had never been saved. He warned us all to steer clear of her, saying that he hoped for the least amount of contact possible. Little did he know that she had come to church late that evening, suffering from a chest cold, and was sitting in a side room in order to minimize the distraction she would cause with her coughing. What she heard Jones say about her was a gift from God: she would have no lingering doubts.

This woman was our friend. Jones's scathing remarks set Annie up to leave the church as well. It was all she could do to contain herself. In the meantime, Joe was sending me tapes from Thieme and the other two pastors. I listened to all three, but the pastor from Dallas quickly got my attention. I soon ordered tapes from his ministry.

Just prior to these developments, God provided us with telltale information about Jones and his family. Annie and I had gotten involved in breeding dogs for sport competition. On one occasion, this required a trip to Minnesota for a breeding session. Jones and his wife, Maude, had two daughters, one of whom was reaching college age. They were interested in sending her to their alma mater in Minnesota, so Annie ended up taking their daughter to Minnesota to explore this possibility. In the process of expressing their thanks to Annie for her efforts, they made some remarks suggesting that college life might be so much fun that their daughter would have no time to listen to tapes of her father's messages. Annie and I were stunned. We had been taught that "inhaling Bible doctrine" was our first priority; anything else was a distant second. Being in church and getting face-to-face teaching was a strong priority over tapes. Annie herself had left a wonderful liberal arts college during her college years and returned home just so that she could be in church every night, and then commute to Purdue University every day. We had discussed the possibility of having children, and we had concluded that, if they were not smart enough to attend college *and* listen to Bible doctrine, they wouldn't go to college—at least not on our dime. We were astonished to hear the Joneses' flippant attitude.

Soon after that, a situation arose in which I needed some help at my office. I decided to ask Maude Jones if she would like to work for me. I could use the help, but I was more interested in figuring out what was missing in my attempts to successfully navigate the Christian life. If there was another set of rules to play by, I needed to know, because I certainly wasn't succeeding playing by the rules of the last nineteen years. I didn't learn much from Maude, but I was able to confirm that Jones was just rewarming what he heard on the tapes from Thieme. At about that time, Jones fell in love with Rush Limbaugh, so I started listening to Limbaugh just to see what he was all about: although he was pleasant and actually moderate compared to what we had been hearing for almost two decades, it was nothing new. Thieme had covered this type of conservatism years before. But now, suddenly, Jones was becoming politically active. We had been taught for all these years that voting

was a waste of time. God simply honored our mental attitude and responded. The value of voting had been destroyed
by the masscs. Now, suddenly, we had to save the country
by voting. As I listened to Limbaugh on long drives back
from sales trips to Cincinnati, it became apparent once
again that I was rushing to church just to hear Limbaugh
regurgitated. This was like going back to first-grade arith-
metic, and it was a great waste of what precious little time
we could call our own in our life.

With the benefits of Charles Stanley, tapes from the
enlightened pastor in Dallas, and more open conversations
with Annie and a trusted friend, I became the hunter instead
of the hunted. I began baiting Maude at work, knowing
that anything I said would get back to Jones. In the past,
those really committed to the regimen of Bible doctrine
thought the only possible option would be another sanctioned church in some distant location. To leave our church
was to leave town, basically tearing up roots and kissing
our previous life good-bye.

For the better part of twenty years, I had entertained the
possibility that I might have the gift of pastor-teacher. If
this were truc, I expected to finish up the education I started
when I first thought this might be a responsibility that I
would have to prepare for. Moving back to the geograph-
ical area of the Fort Wayne church was also attractive. I
started dropping hints in front of Maude of this plan. At the
same time, the Dallas pastor was teaching about a kind and
compassionate God. This was earth-shaking as far as we
were concerned. After what Annie and I had been through,
we desperately needed to hear this. Reflecting his message,
the Dallas pastor's demeanor stood in stark contrast to the
mean demeanor we had dealt with for years.

The inner pressure intensified. Then one evening, we received the anticipated feedback. Jones started into a rant. He spoke of what a silly notion it would be for a couple of reversionists to consider leaving town under the guise of having the gift of pastor-teacher and preparing for some future ministry. Everyone in church knew of whom he was speaking. Not only did he have no respect for the idea that I might have to submit to God with respect to his gifting me, he also labeled Annie and me reversionists, likely just a few steps from the "sin unto death."

Memorial Day, 1993, dawned sunny and warm. Annie and I had the day off to putter in our garden and generally enjoy the fourteen-acre hobby farm the Lord had blessed us with a few years before. I brewed some coffee and sat back in my easy chair to listen to a tape from the Dallas pastor. Annie was up and soon out the door to enjoy our dogs and the coming of spring. I sipped on my coffee and listened. The tape finished, and I inserted the next one in a series the pastor had made. As I listened, I couldn't believe what I heard. The contrast became greater and greater. It was truly light versus darkness.

Annie returned from outdoors through the sliding glass door in the kitchen. She peeked her head into the living room. With a slight hint of frustration over the lack of my availability and the nice day I was wasting, she queried me: "Are you coming outdoors today or not?" I looked at her with what was likely a blank stare and replied, "Not for a while, I need to listen to another tape." I could see her disappointment as she turned and quietly retreated back outdoors.

With a refilled coffee cup and tape player, I soon heard what finally, after years, tipped the scales in our favor. There was no need to leave town in order to leave church. I wasn't a reversionist—I was simply longing for God. If I did not go back into church, where I might be dissuaded by something from the pulpit, I was done! I jumped from my chair and ran out to detail my mindset and my plan to Annie.

I had been raised under stricter authority than she had. If I went back and heard something that gave me pause, I might have to sit there indefinitely to get past it. I hoped she could glide into church one more time, ignore what she heard, and gather up our Bibles, tape recorder, clothes, and whatever else we had stashed around the two seats we had occupied for the last ten years. I couldn't afford to take that chance. If Annie felt uncomfortable, we could always ask someone in her family to bring us our Bibles and family heirlooms. But she had no problem going one more time. She might be asked where I was, but she was up to the task. Now it was time to enjoy a few hours outside before the rest of the day escaped us.

The Good Shepherd had been ministering to our wounds until we were healthy enough to be moved. Psalm 18 is a beautiful picture of what happens when we cry to God for help and he has to deliver us from our enemies. Indeed, God shook our world and everyone in our periphery when it was his time to rescue us.

CHAPTER 9
SUPER GRACE

And the grace of our Lord overflowed for me with the faith and love that are in Christ Jesus.
—1 Timothy 1:14

Stand fast therefore in the liberty by which Christ has made us free, and do not be entangled again with a yoke of bondage.
—Galatians 5:1

We were out! We were finally out! We had been set free! We were a little apprehensive about what might happen next, because Annie's family also attended the church. We were concerned that they might be pressured from the pulpit because of our departure. Also, Maude Jones still worked for me. Was she going to be a problem? We expected a full rant from the pulpit. We were now reversionists on a nonstop path to the "sin unto death."

I immediately called my father-in-law so that he would hear the news from us. We didn't want him to be blindsided from the pulpit about our status. He told me nothing would change in our relationship. He suggested that everyone must be free to chart his or her own course. Maude gave her two-week notice, and soon my office returned to normal. Meanwhile, Annie and I were in a state of euphoria. We were carried aloft by the experience of true freedom. But this was no teenage night on the town: our freedom was accompanied by some serious capacity for life. We looked at life with wonder and amazement.

I don't think that there are many who have escaped the tyranny of communism who were happier than we were at that moment. If we had just touched down in the good ol' U.S. of A, we would have kissed the ground. Our experience was less public but no less real: the chains of *mental* tyranny began to break. Once we were on the outside, we were able to see the cult for the charade it had become. Many stories have been written about those who had somehow escaped communist regimes and been granted the freedom to continue their lives in the United States. But often these stories end with great sadness. After exerting immense effort and taking great risk to attain their freedom, they find it overwhelming to have to make the decisions that freedom requires. After a short time, they return to the oppression of a tyrannical regime, where someone else is making their decisions for them, often from cradle to grave.

Such was not our case. The Lord had healed us to the point that there was no turning back. It was time to move forward. While we listened to tapes from the Dallas pastor, we checked out a doctrinal church nearly sixty miles from our home. They were in a reforming mode, a process made necessary by the exaggerated influence Thieme had had on them. It seemed that they were trying to make their corrections within the confines of previously held protocols. We hoped that we were beyond such a regimen, so we set our sights on *normal churches* closer to home. We visited a Baptist church and, after Annie made a few inquiries as to their doctrinal position, we decided to attend regularly.

We had been taught that human love apart from the Holy Spirit was undesirable. I don't know what these folks at the Baptist church had, but it felt good. They seemed to genuinely enjoy each other, and they welcomed us into their fellowship. Annie and I enjoyed the full menu of opportunity within the church: we attended the three services per week; I got involved with the teenagers as their youth pastor; and both of us joined the choir. After the service on a Wednesday or Sunday night, we would often join the pastor and our new friend, Dave, in conversations about God and his wonders. These conversations would start at about 8:00 p.m. and might last until after 11:00 p.m., when, for the third or fourth time, one of us would suggest that we ought to get some sleep before work the next morning. We were living large! We were living in the amazement of God's blessings.

God's blessings kept overflowing. A conversation with my father-in-law reaped an enormous harvest. They had joined the cult as middle-aged adults and hadn't been as easily influenced as the younger set. Still, I knew what his attendance meant to his family. I told him that the best thing he and my mother-in-law could do for their grandchildren would be to leave. He looked at his wife; her look left no need for a verbal reply. They soon left. They were immediately followed out the door by the rest of the family. My three sisters-in-law and their families, which included eight young children, were out. The church, which had had about forty attendees, lost twenty in two years — sixteen of them in the last few months.

The cult never recovered. Another handful of attendees left within the next couple of years. Years later, Jones apparently closed the doors when Maude died. He put his house up for sale and moved out of town, leaving the last few members to fend for themselves.

Our lives continued to be enriched by our new church. Soon Annie's parents joined us there. My father-in-law was so enamored with the pastor and his demeanor that he told me that he truly loved the man. These were no insignificant words for a man to speak about another man, especially after having spent twenty years in the macho culture we had just escaped. Holy Spirit was busy debunking myths in our souls and replacing them with truth. One of the greatest comforts the Spirit brought to our lives was the biblical truth concerning marriage. There was no such thing as a biblical doctrine of "right man" and "right woman." The Bible establishes marriage as the institution designed by God to protect the love of a man and a woman, and consequently to protect the family. Biblically, a man or a woman is free to marry any opposite-sex partner they desire. The only caveat for the believer in Jesus Christ is that his or her partner must also be a believer. Obviously, this also rejects any incestuous or other relationships that would create disharmony.

What an incredible relief that was. I hadn't married the wrong woman after all! I hadn't stolen someone else's bride! And I wasn't under any discipline from God for my choice. We could expect God to do the most for us in our marriage. Annie and I could have a beautiful future together. What an awesome gift from an awesome God!

Another area of our lives that had really suffered during the cult years was related to our finances and our jobs. We had always been kept off-balance in pursuit of any career advancement. In the cult, if you were not police or military personnel, you were expected to be in church every time it met. There was no sense thinking that you could take a job that would cause you to leave town or the church. We had been told that we were going to die in the cult church.

Over the years, many who have sat at our table have lauded my culinary skills. After being a cook during my stint in the army, I had worked with my oldest brother in his pizza shop. Now, twenty years later, I was in my forties and had spent years working in the prepackaged sandwich business. I found the food side of the business quite unimaginative; but if the business was well run, it could be quite lucrative.

Randy, my fellow sales manager, and I had entertained the idea of buying the central Indiana portion of our boss's business. When we broached the subject to him, he told us to give him a price. He recommended that we go to others in the industry and have them give us an idea what his business was worth. We pursued this course and came back to him with a price. Initially, he seemed very pleased with the offer and said he would get back to us. After a few weeks, however, he returned to our offices and informed us that his accountant had nixed the idea. The accountant told him he couldn't afford to sell off part of his business. We then suggested that he franchise the territory we were interested in, and we would purchase sandwiches from him. It sounded like a plan until he reminded me that I wasn't happy with the deteriorating quality of his product. He was correct, and I was certainly glad he alerted us.

It looked like our plans had failed and everything was going to return to the mediocrity that had become the norm. Randy decided to look for employment elsewhere. And I could tell that my boss was growing weary of me. He'd bought the business from the original owner six or seven years earlier, but he had never understood food or people. He was ruining a good business. In his view, part of the solution was to get rid of me.

Randy and I recalled that one of the other sandwich companies would sell us a truck and sandwiches. If we could find the customers, we would have a business that cost us little more than sweat equity and the security of our paychecks. After talking with our wives and the Lord, we decided to take the risk. It was by no means a sure thing. The business would have to succeed in two to four weeks, or we would be out of money. And we would be competing with our former boss. Annie's employment could cover the house payment, but we only had about two thousand dollars in savings to work with. I was losing my company car, which left us with only a high-mileage pickup for Annie to make the eighty-mile round trip to work each day.

Memorial Day weekend, 1995, arrived sunny and cool. Randy and his wife picked me up, and we made the three-hour trip to Illinois to get our truck and a load of sandwiches. With laughter and excitement, we drove back to Indiana and began calling on our former boss's customers. We were met with exceptional enthusiasm, considering that it was a Saturday and no one was expecting us. By Saturday evening we had called on about twenty-five accounts; of those, we were able to secure eighteen immediately as our exclusive customers. It had been a good day. Another four or five told us to wait a week so they could sell down their inventory. We headed to our homes to spend the evening and Sunday in our normal pursuits.

Back in the truck bright and early Memorial Day morning, we headed to Indianapolis, where the customers were more familiar with me. We called on thirty-some accounts on Monday and about the same on Tuesday. With the exception of two stores, they all came with us. We had called on ninety accounts and over eighty were ours. We worked Wednesday and Thursday of that week until we ran out of sandwiches. By that time, we had secured a hundred and twenty-five accounts. We had had immediate success! Although we had to deal with several obstacles over the course of the next few months, some of great magnitude, our business made money even in the first week and every week thereafter. I sat down that next Saturday morning on my outdoor deck and smiled at the Lord. We had been told in the cult that, when you had matured in Bible doctrine, the Lord could give you "super grace" blessings. In twenty years, it had never happened. Not even close. Now, as I was supposedly dying the sin unto death, it had happened. Grace was overflowing. We had knocked down all of these accounts just by asking for their business. The people knew us, but I was certainly no super salesman. This was the Lord blessing us abundantly above and beyond what I could ask or imagine. I sat there and reveled in his blessings and his care. I did matter to him!

CHAPTER 10
THE GOD OF SECOND OR THIRD CHANCES

There are three things which are too wonderful for me, yes, four which I do not understand: the way of an eagle in the air, the way of a serpent on a rock, the way of a ship in the midst of the sea, and the way of a man with a virgin (young woman).
—Proverbs 30:18-19

When a man has taken a new wife, he shall not go out to war or be charged with any business; he shall be free at home for one year and bring happiness to his wife whom he has taken.
—Deuteronomy 24:5

I am a hopeless romantic. If there was one thing I wanted to succeed at, it was marriage. But nothing about me suggested that I would. I was an introvert, either by nature or by conditioning—or both. In second grade, my school principal had taught me to read of heroes and of a life much bigger than the one I was born into. I developed high expectations of men, women, myself, and others. Six older siblings made relating to kids my own age, be they male or female, quite a task by the time I was a teen. My dad was a closet intellectual, and I enjoyed the depth of his thoughts. Between eighth grade and my freshman year of high school, I spent the summer at the home of one of my sisters, with her husband and two children. When an anticipated job fell through, I spent the summer smoking cigarettes and playing bridge with her and her lady friends. An occasional beer with my brother-in-law and the air-traffic-controller next door made shoehorning back into my little Dutch Reformed world a cause for blisters.

When it came to women, no one had ever qualified, except for the young woman I had found sitting beside me at Indiana University. But when I'd accompanied my friend Joe to his church, there sat Annie, and she had a vibe that gave me pause. I realized that I had been looking for someone to trust my soul with, and she might possibly be the first one to ever qualify.

Marriage had turned me into a hapless romantic: I was a total failure and still longing for someone to share my soul with. This wasn't going to happen in the cult, because in our ten years of marriage, it had been my general responsibility to crush my wife under the weight of impossible legalism and stupidity, to the point where she would have no motivation to share a glass of tea, let alone her soul. Now, at forty-plus and free, there was finally hope. The God police were gone. Everything we had was ours, either given to us by our gracious God or something he was allowing us to develop from his assets in our souls. As the constraints and the crap washed away, Annie gave me a peek at her mind and soul. In fact, she began to engage in a way that told me she could go deep with me: that she could understand my thoughts, plumb the depths of those thoughts, and respond in an intelligent way that no one else ever had. She understood, and she was interested. This was incredible, especially considering that, for most people, being around my intense personality more than an hour or so would make them feel like they had been in an enclosure where someone started up the engine of a

300-mile-per-hour dragster. Somehow, she found my soul interesting enough to endure the intensity.

As for me—I was mesmerized. Annie's mind was a mental playground for me. Her soul was a mystery that engaged my full attention as I tried to piece together the person she was revealing in a peekaboo fashion. Suddenly, a hundred-mile drive became a marathon session of love-making, fully clothed, in the front seat of our car at seventy miles-per-hour. It was *better* than sex for me to be finally finding communion with the person I chose to be the love of my life. Every facet of her life that I was privileged to observe became a blessing. After working the ground for her, seeing her gentle hands planting seed, and embracing the mystery of God's abundance—all of it was experiencing a joyful harvest in our garden and in the Eden of our lives.

I built a whelping box, and she played midwife to our German shepherd bitch and her litter of pups. Annie's controlled exterior kept the impending mother calm in her hour of distress. To see Annie aid in the birth of ten or twelve pups after the midnight hour, already exhausted by the wait, was to see the natural sacrifice that caused me to speculate on the what-ifs of our life had she become the mother of our children.

Building a business together offered a whole other vista. She took on the challenges from the first day, becoming our bookkeeper while holding down a full-time job to sustain us. Her painstaking efforts only continued to blossom into a totally engaged partner. Slowly but surely, my life and my marriage were becoming what I had always dreamed of, and it all spoke to a gracious and miracle-working God.

⌐•⌐

During a winter holiday retreat with some folks from the doctrinal church on the mend, we were blessed with a special speaker who had a prison ministry in Georgia. He mentioned that one of the poor black prisoners had responded to his message by saying, "God loves even me!" My first response was one of happiness and sympathy. I was happy for this poor man. I was also sympathetic, reflecting that it took prison for him to discover that God loved him.

The retreat soon ended, and I was back to my normal work routine. But the poor black prisoner's words hung in my mind: "God loves even me!" I began to realize that I was poorer than that poor man. I wasn't in a physical prison, but I lived in a prison of my own, a prison where I hadn't experienced the love of God. At first it was hard to admit how truly impoverished I was. I tried to argue with myself that I knew God loved me. It was an argument God wouldn't let me win.

Pop-rock music — indeed, most music — had been severely condemned in the cult. This had created a twenty-year gap in my mental music library. Now, as I was looking for music I might enjoy, I came across "I Want to Know What Love Is" by Foreigner." The lyrics that I heard sounded like a modern-day Psalm: the lyricist refers to a life of heartache and pain, and he declares that he has traveled far in his attempts to change his lonely life. His anthem becomes one I could easily hear King David, the psalmist, crying out to God. The singer pleads, with enormous angst, that he wants to know what love is, and he wants an unidentified person to show him. And he wants to experience this love *inside*!

I was now in my forties, and I hadn't experienced God's love. I had had two or three experiences in my childhood when I had felt loved, but they were momentary and diminished by other experiences that showed little regard for my soul. At twenty, I followed the gospel message of God's love for everyone only to have it turn into a cult that said God couldn't love anyone. It wasn't as if something were terribly wrong with my life—quite the contrary. I loved Annie deeply. On the spiritual front, the two of us continued to enjoy the freedom to become the people God intended us to be. There were plenty of kinks in our souls, but I was confident that God was up to the task. We both seemed willing to allow him to do his handiwork.

Our business continued to grow—exponentially. Randy and I split the business as we had previously agreed to. We would run our businesses similarly, but we would maintain our own separate and exclusive territories. I made the decision to buy a new route truck with a refrigerated body. If I wasn't committed before, I was by then. With a new car for Annie, and soon a new sales vehicle for the business, there were plenty of bills to pay. Not to worry: we were quickly becoming the dominant sandwich company in central Indiana. I hired a man to help me in sales and route work. Annie, already helping with the books, quit her job and joined the business full-time. We were making plans to lease a building and start producing the grab-and-go cold sandwiches part of our menu.

Much of my family, from whom I had been mostly estranged during my years in the cult, were back in my life. A number of them made the 150-mile trip to witness Annie and me receive believer's baptism. Even though we had pretty well checked off any plans for children, I enjoyed the warm and fuzzy feeling of pseudo-fatherhood. I would sit among a litter of German shepherd puppies just a few weeks old and watch the proud behavior of their mother as she shared the experience with us. God was good. Life was good. Marriage was good. Church was good. Family was good. Business was good. Friends were good. I figured everything could only get better and better.

I made what turned out to be the most crucial decision of my life. My decision decades before to trust in Jesus had changed my eternal destiny, but nothing had affected my temporal life like this decision would. I went before the Lord and told him that, whatever it took, I wanted to know what love is: I wanted God to show me. Some days I wish I could have those words back! Some days.

CHAPTER 11
AN AFFAIR OF THE HEART

The Lord gave and the Lord has taken away. Blessed be the name of the Lord.
—Job 1:21

Our lives continued to be busy and joyful. New discoveries in the Lord happened regularly, and our daily routine allowed Annie and me to work side by side each morning, building sandwiches with our employees. Each afternoon Annie retired to her office to do paperwork or home to engage in various activities. I would spend the rest of my day overseeing all the other aspects of our business. On Saturdays, Annie would make the two-hour journey to the dog club to train for sport competition. I would usually spend the morning getting all our receipts from the week in the bank. I could then spend time at the neighborhood restaurant with the local farmers and retirees. Afterward, I would return home to enjoy time outdoors or prepare for the next morning's youth meeting or the small-group meeting at our house that very night.

But then things began to change. I was asked to let a missionary who had recently returned to the church show me how to facilitate the young people's group. Apparently, he wanted his two sons to get something I wasn't giving. I had previously encouraged a deacon's daughter to check out what the Bible had to say about alcoholic beverages, after she had made a judgment about someone's soul based on his or her consumption of such drinks. I told her she might discover that the first miracle our Lord performed involved producing an alcoholic beverage. I soon found that many in the congregation felt that their position on alcohol defined their life as Christians—more than the person of Christ. I had crossed into a no man's land, and the pastor—whom I greatly admired—didn't defend me. I decided to resign my position as the youth pastor, and to return to the enjoyment of the pastor's Sunday-morning Bible study.

Soon thereafter, our route driver quit for a job that better suited him. It had always been difficult to find an adequate person to do this job. And if you didn't do so, the wrong person could destroy your business in a matter of months. As I searched for new help, I was forced to work from 4:15 a.m. to anywhere from eight o'clock to ten o'clock at night every weekday. After months of this, it became a matter of just putting one foot in front of the other. The highlight of my life became waking up at 2:30 a.m. for a bathroom run and discovering that I still had about two hours to sleep.

Meanwhile, Annie was left to work with just the women in our commissary. They were all in their forties and enjoyed a certain rapport. At some point their conversations began to acknowledge the deliverymen who frequented our business. Suddenly, Annie was into guy-watching. Although it seemed innocuous, it was something I had never seen in her before.

At about the same time, she started to receive emails to our shared account from a fellow dog-club member, a man who accompanied his wife and their two young sons to dog training. The content of his emails was innocent enough, but the tone expressed an availability a married man probably shouldn't have toward a married woman. He had a willingness to invest in my wife. I told Annie to tell him that, if he kept it up, I would have to shoot him. She couldn't see what I as a man could see, but she told him just the same. He was shocked—shocked that she and I had a shared email account! I think he was a little scared, too.

At about that time, our Saturday night small-group gathering began to disintegrate. The older folks who had enjoyed our freshness and enthusiasm were put off by anything that fell outside their comfort zone. To think that the song "Spirit in the Sky" might have an evangelistic message appalled them. They retreated back to their bastions of Baptist thinking. We continued with just three of us, and it was a wonderful time, but we had become suspect among the larger church group. Although our best friend, Dave, continued with us on Saturday nights, he had sought out a different church to attend. He felt that our pastor was giving the older crowd a pass on any topic that might upset them.

I agreed with Dave. Even though I love this pastor and still consider myself his friend, I thought he allowed Baptist convictions to have more sway at times than the person of Jesus. Who knows—he may have grown weary of his efforts to affect these folks after more than twenty years of ministry to them. Or his Baptist upbringing may have left him blind to their need to grow. With Dave's departure, the dynamics changed: within the congregation, conversations of awe and the splendor of God faded away. Others tried to join in, but there was a more legalistic and diminishing feel to it. This had an immediate effect on me. After forty years of being misled in the name of God, I was in no mood to be tyrannized or see a drift toward some of the false teachings of John Calvin. When the pastor seemed to ally himself with these perspectives, Annie and I thought it might be time to look for a new church home.

We started attending churches even closer to home. When one seemed to be a poor fit because of doctrinal issues, we found ourselves taking some time to restart the search. This was a new reality in my life. For forty-five years I had attended church two to six times a week. With my ninety-hour-a-week work schedule, it was a relief to have Sundays off. I could sleep in, sit in front of the talking heads with my cup of coffee, and feel refreshed by Sunday afternoon. I could spend some time with Annie and the dogs and enjoy the outdoors. I could read books that I had neglected for months. The time away from a church influence also allowed me to survey my own private thoughts. Our business was all-consuming. I could see it just turning into a long-term money machine. But I wanted to be about more than counting my money in old age. So my thoughts turned to what would give life purpose once we had gained financial independence.

Though the business was successful, we continued to have a critical lack of help, despite our prayers. Our oppressive work schedules left us suffering from different forms of exhaustion. Mine was more physical—Annie's more emotional. What was once a wonderful blessing was becoming quite burdensome. Other business dynamics were also at play. The company that helped in our start-up was now interested in buying us out. If they were to refuse to sell us sandwiches, we would have to have an immediate plan to make all of our own. This would be an expensive investment. Labor remained scarce. The unemployment rate in the county was under 1 percent. Even bad help was hard to find. The business did not stir our imagination. Was God calling us to something else?

As I looked and listened for something from God, it was Annie's voice that I heard next. We had made plans for a long weekend. We were to meet my sisters and brothers-in-law the next morning in Indianapolis for the Gaithers' "Praise Gathering." On the eve of this occasion, Annie made a quiet but startling announcement: she told me that she had rather inadvertently fallen in love with another man and probably wanted a divorce.

I was dumbstruck. Though I was surprisingly calm externally, I was dumbstruck. Annie had spoken of divorce before, but it had never involved another person or another love. There were a lot of things my wife was and was not, but this was something I never expected. I knew that Annie was a sinner. Still, I think it's fair to say that this was completely uncharacteristic behavior from her. Some people's sins precede them, some follow them. When you are around a person for a while, either casually or intimately, you get a sense of where their weaknesses lie. Some are gossips, some are worriers, some are anxious, some are rude, some are self-centered, some even have self-destructive compulsions. But Annie had never been one to seek the illicit affections of another. She had a personal honor code: it included sexual purity and loyalty. But when she said that she had *inadvertently* fallen in love with another man, it had a certain ring of truth to it.

My emotions roared within me. How did this happen? Who is this guy? How did he pull this off? Are they sleeping together? Is she serious? I needed answers, but I didn't want them. Our marital life had gotten progressively better. Why now? For the last seven or eight years, our lives had finally made sense. I just wanted all this to go away. But it wasn't going to. She was serious. The more she thought about it, the more serious she became. Problems like these have roots, and this problem had long ones. Some roots run shallow along the ground and interweave with every aspect of our lives; others run deep, so deep that if we were to uproot them, something surely would be killed.

So, what was the problem? According to Annie, she didn't love me. And never had. Seventeen years into marriage, and she had come to a point of freedom where she was able to acknowledge this out loud. She wanted out. In my seventeen years of marriage, on the other hand, I had come to adore her. Not for who I thought she was, not for who I had hoped she was, not for who she was in so many ways. Rather, in my failure to find the woman I wanted, I had in humble desperation asked the Lord to show me how to love her. And did he ever! By the grace of God, she had become the joy of my life. On God's terms, he began to show me a woman who fit me. Not the way I expected, but better.

There was much we had been cheated out of in our twenty years in the cult. Once out, I could rationalize the results as being worth the investment. What I had learned both negatively and positively in those twenty years was a springboard to a bigger life. I figured that most people don't do much serious living between twenty and forty. Most get caught up in jobs, spouses, children, and mundane distractions that don't provide much of an accelerant to their search for God. We had been so abused that our desire to find the true God was intense. The only thing I had deeply regretted—besides my boorish behavior during those years—was not honoring God with the children he desired from us.

On the other hand, Annie had another regret that burned in her heart. She had been intimidated into dating me lest she miss her "right man." In the process, she had never fallen in love with me. When her younger sister once queried her during our courtship if she was in love, she responded that she was "in like." Apparently, this was as far as she ever got. In the downward spiral at the beginning of our marriage, we were both robbed of the emotions we desired toward each other. But, in her case, those emotions were forever elusive. Finally, seventeen years later, she was surprised as this guy caused them to be awakened within her for the first time. What was she to do if she were to be true to her own soul? To be honest, it seemed that she must live a life without me.

Thus began a year of animated suspense. Our marriage and much of who we were hung in the balance. Knowing how the Lord had changed me over the seventeen years of our marriage, I had confidence that he was going to use our situation to draw us closer to him and to each other. No one relishes a battle with evil, but Annie and I were soldiers. We had fought some of life's greatest battles together and emerged victorious. This was no time to abandon her. To do so would be to abandon a fellow soldier on the battlefield. In her state of confusion and emotion, she had fired on our marriage and me, and had hit us point blank. We were on relational life-support. What should I do?

I got before the Lord. I knew I needed more love and I needed it quick. I had found my love depleted previously and had asked God for his help. He had answered me with a love for Annie I'd never known. This love allowed me to see and enjoy new vistas of her person. Now I was going to need a love for her and a love for my enemy (the man she had fallen in love with) that went beyond my expectations.

CHAPTER 12

SHE LOVES ME, SHE
LOVES ME NOT

*But I say to you, love your enemies, bless those who curse you,
do good to those who hate you, and pray for those who spite-
fully use you and persecute you.*
—Matthew 5:44

I have always been a highly driven person, and not
inclined to be patient. If there is such a thing as a type-A
personality, I fit the mold. A route business serving convenience stores does not lend itself toward patience. To make
money, you had to make time. As I got older, I wearied of
some of the stress I had created in my life. I decided to slow
down and relax and get home when I got home, instead
of pushing all day. What was routinely a twelve-hour day
might turn into fourteen, but it seemed worth it to come
home relaxed. My efforts resulted in an extra half hour on
the road, but my state of mind was much improved.

The real secret to my traveling success was what God
had whispered in my noggin: "Pray for them, Garry, pray
for your enemies." The Lord was referring to my fellow
motorists, who typically frazzled me. My first response was
that I couldn't really classify them as my enemies. But the
Lord shot back: "The way you treat them certainly qualifies
them as such!" I'd been had. And so, instead of standing on

top of people in traffic and driving with a scorched-earth policy, I relaxed and prayed that God would send them his Son if they were unbelievers and send them his blessings if they were believers. I discovered the genius of Jesus's admonition to pray for your enemies and do good to those who persecute you. When you do that, they no longer own you. They no longer have power over you!

This practice made dealing with my wife's paramour possible. Everything within me wanted to destroy him, but the Lord gave me the ability to pray for him. And as I did pray for him, he, too, went from being my enemy to a fellow brother in Christ whose desires had gotten the best of him. I was no less displeased, but he wasn't controlling my life. I could turn the majority of my attention to prayer for Annie and me, and to determine whether there was any hope for our marriage.

I have never done any illicit drugs, but I understand that they have a powerful pull. When I would hear Annie's thoughts under the influence of being *in love* for the first time, it made me wonder, "What is the stronger stimulant— drugs or love?" She was on a high that no one could talk her down from. Nonetheless, talking ensued—a lot of talking. Annie and I would engage in conversation regarding her state of mind. Her statement that she had never loved me was almost more than I could bear, but it was also confusing. She hadn't really behaved as if she didn't love me, though she had a reticence about her that I had chalked up to her singular personality. She was somewhat aloof and soft-spoken with most people. Compared to some of her interactions with other men when she was single, I felt fortunate to have had effective conversations with her. Later, when we engaged in counseling, our counselor said that she had never experienced anyone whose responses were

71

as slow to develop as Annie's. She was a highly intelligent woman, and she was also a perfectionist. Her father had said that there was no good reason to stick your foot in your mouth. Therefore, the words that came out of her mouth were always well measured.

I had come to accept the fact that Annie was never going to be carefree or outgoing in her expression of love for me. But gentle kisses, relaxed smiles, holding my hand in her lap when we drove to a favorite restaurant—these were things I thought expressed her affections for me. She took care and pride in shopping for special gifts for me. A suit or leather jacket for Christmas may have been modeled by a salesman she thought to be my size, just to assure her that she was bringing home something that was perfect for me. As our conversations continued, it became apparent that she was not angry with me, nor was she disappointed in my person. Her ringing words, which I never forgot, were: "Garry, I think you would make someone a pretty good husband now, just not me." Our marriage simply was not the relationship she had wanted from the very beginning, and after seventeen years and an accidental love affair, it was time to do something about it. At this point she didn't know what that might be. She wasn't ready to bail out of the marriage, though she was long past any desire to make it work. She was in a no man's land surrounded by hard choices on either side. What was the right thing to do? Annie suggested that we see a marriage counselor. I was too dumb to respond well, and I still carried the aftereffects of being taught that such counseling was evil—as well as my own doubts about its legitimacy. But after some protesting, I agreed to seek Christian counsel. My hopes were that any Christian counselor would be able to help my wife understand that her desire for a divorce was not biblical. This turned out to be wishful thinking on my part: Annie already knew that her desires were not biblical. But having escaped a biblical cult after twenty years, she was way past settling for biblical. She needed someone who understood her. She needed someone to listen to her soul. And I was thankful that we could find a female counselor who could listen— and did. Over the next nine months, Annie and I received some real insight and wisdom.

I started looking for whatever other help I could find that would not announce our failing marriage to those who knew us. I started buying books on love, marriage, and divorce. As the pile of books next to my easy chair grew, Annie would read them after I went to bed. She stumbled on one by Dr. Phil that was not unequivocally opposed to divorce. Although Dr. Phil is a Christian, he couched his words in such a way that it gave Annie the freedom to further consider the divorce option. Soon she met with her family and explained where she was with respect to our marriage. She was told that, whatever was going to happen, they would fully support her. And her friends, even though they disagreed with her divorce plans, were not going to leave or forsake her either.

As our counseling continued, the counselor advised me that the two of us should meet with her in separate sessions. She thought that there was no reason for me to sit there and have my wife verbally beat me up. Soon Annie's sessions became more about her and less about us. She started working out the kinks that remained from twenty years in the cult. Over the months she would zig and zag on marriage; but ultimately, she had to be true to her own soul. She had never gotten to where she really wanted to marry me, she had no desire to remain married, and she would rather spend the rest of her life single than spend it in a marriage she didn't enjoy. She had never been *in love* with me, and somehow that became the ultimate criterion. Nothing else mattered. She had experienced the high of being in love, and it hadn't happened with me. After almost eighteen years of marriage, she finally made the decision that she wished she had made eighteen years before. She was ending what, for her, had never fully engaged her heart.

CHAPTER 13
CRASH LANDING

*And we know all things work together for good to those who
love God, to those who are the called according to his purpose.*
—Romans 8:28

The sandwich company that had helped Randy and me
get started in our business was now aggressively pur-
suing us. They wanted to buy us out and were willing to
pay a handsome price. If we didn't sell to them, they were
going to come into our territory anyway. I knew I couldn't
effectively run my business without Annie. She had been a
great help in the business. And considering my emotional
state after years of long hours, coupled with the thought of
her leaving me, made me realize that it would be impossible
for me to carry on. We accepted their offer.

With no motive to stay in our house, I agreed to move
out. There seemed to be little reason to stay in the area.
Even though I had a handful of good friends locally, they
would not be enough to sustain me. I had put my all into
a failing relationship for eighteen years. Simultaneously, I
had invested all my physical energy into our business for
the last five years. I was emotionally and physically spent.
I had no idea what to do. What in heaven's name was God
calling me to, and where on earth was he leading me?

What I really needed was a hole to crawl into, a place
to hide my embarrassment, shame, and pain. I had no

idea where to go, but I had the financial freedom to consider many options. Maybe I could return to college after twenty-five years and prepare for God to use me in some yet unseen way. With little hope that I could hold things together in our marriage, that appeared to be a good option. Nick, my best friend from our childhood days, made the trek down to help move what remained of my earthly possessions over a hundred miles to a rental apartment just off campus at Grace College. After we had lunch and unloaded the truck, he left me to embark on my new life.

I soon was off to classes as a forty-eight-year-old among those who could have been my children: almost everyone was eighteen to twenty, and that just added to my sense of isolation. As I attended class after class, I tried to focus, but it just wasn't working. All day long and into the night— even in the middle of my restless sleep—my mind tried to figure out how to save our marriage. Our counselor had thought that Annie would likely come around and want to save the marriage. Annie had said she wanted to see if she would miss me, so I clung to a thread of hope that things would somehow change for the better.

As time went on, I became more forlorn; I missed my wife terribly. Although she had cut off sexual relations nearly a year earlier, it was the soul relationship that I now missed the most. I had cared for her, prayed for her, and thought of her in the most intense way for the past year. Now she was gone and likely never coming back. What would I become without her? I was homesick. I no longer had the opportunity to express my love and affection, and I was beginning to fear life without her. I might not make it. I was approaching panic.

I kept going to classes, but I was starting to lose it. I knew I could never pass any midterm exams. My efforts to feed myself were getting more desperate. I was a good cook, but I didn't feel like cooking. I was losing the energy to take care of myself. When I went grocery shopping, the supermarket felt like a dungeon. The store was well lit, but the drop-down, dark-wood framing devoured the light. It was hard to be there because I was in my own dungeon of darkness and pain. To shop there was to intensify my sense of imprisonment. A greeting from someone I knew was enough to throw me into a psychosis. Was I free or was I in chains? I interacted with my two closest sisters at that time, but their love was not enough to sustain me. I had been functioning for a year on reserve tanks. I had hopes that the Lord would soft-land my life, even though all controls had virtually been destroyed. Instead, I staggered around as though I were the lone mangled survivor of an airplane crash. All that mattered to me had disappeared or been destroyed. My marriage was nowhere to be found. Our quiet hobby farm, which ran for a quarter mile along a creek secluded in the woods, was nowhere in sight. The dogs we had bred and raised were no longer mine. The business that had been founded in faith and prospered by the Lord had been sold. My eighteen-hour days of purpose and enjoyment were strewn in the wreckage around me.

My soul was in an inferno of uncontrollable pain, and I needed to find a way to die. I had suffered pain and loss before, but things were different this time. In the past, I could always say that my pain was my own fault; somehow, that had its own comforts. Other than that, I just sucked it up, strapped it on, and moved forward, carrying the pain along with all the other baggage I had accumulated in the first forty-eight years of living. This time the formula would not work. Nor did it seem that looking for more of God would work. I didn't know how to look for more of God.

More of God—less of self—had always worked in the past. I was no fledgling Christian: I had had a lot of downs and some ups in my first forty-some years. But I had begun to find the God I had been looking for. It had become an ever more enjoyable life with him. Now this! I thought this kind of darkness was reserved for hell. I called our marriage counselor on our eighteenth wedding anniversary and told her I thought I better commit suicide. I could find no way to go on living with the jumble in my head. If it continued to get worse, I knew I would soon need a rubber room. I could not see any way to make life work.

So much for the wonderful quote in Romans 8:28 that, for those who love God, all things work together for good. I had actually expected Annie to quote this passage as some rationale that divorce would be of small consequence to me when she left. Together we had been intense students of the Bible for twenty-five years, for thirty-plus years if you added everything up. I knew that if she did quote it, I couldn't refute her. Well, maybe I should have studied a little longer. It was the rest of that chapter in Romans that I was now experiencing.

CHAPTER 14
STAYING ALIVE

Who has directed the Spirit of the Lord, or as his counselor
has taught him? With whom did he take counsel, and who
instructed him and showed him the way of understanding?
Behold the nations are as a drop in the bucket.
—Isaiah 40:3,14a, 15

My marriage counselor quickly inquired whether I had a suicide plan. I told her I didn't. This seemed to reassure her that I wasn't yet standing on the edge of the ledge, so to speak, and she suggested that I come down to Indianapolis to see her. In fact, I was closer to the edge than she might have thought. I only needed some intestinal fortitude and then a method would be follow-through. A pastor I had counseled with implied that God might not forgive suicide, so I had to review my long-held beliefs on the grace of God and eternal security. Thinking was getting really hard to do. I headed for Indianapolis with the hope I could still drive the hundred and fifty miles to see her.

I did make it down to her office, but it soon became apparent what terrible shape I was in. She counseled with me, gave me a book to read, and prayed with me. As soon as I left, I suspect she called Annie to see if there was anyone who would care for me. By the time I returned to northern Indiana, my youngest sister, Patricia, was calling and encouraging me to stay with her for a while. Annie had spoken with her and had told her about my deterio-rating condition. I didn't have much hope that staying with Patricia would help, but it was my best option. The next day I packed what I would need for an extended time and headed off to my sister's home in the Chicago suburbs.

It was good to see my sister, but it did nothing to diminish my mounting anxieties. I didn't know much about real grief, but it felt like fear. I started having bad dreams because I was afraid of my fearful feelings. It was getting hard to eat. My stomach was in such turmoil that it could hardly stand to have anything in it. Although I had been somewhat overweight, I was losing weight at an alarming rate. I tried to eat just so that Patricia would have less reason to be anxious.

My sister had a two-bedroom apartment, but not two beds, so I started out sleeping on the mattress of the hide-away sofa that I pulled out and put on the living-room floor. I would finally fall into a restless sleep at two or three in the morning. When I woke up at daylight and began thinking again, I told myself that I would get up when I figured out how to live life without Annie. My failed efforts to figure it out left me glued to the mattress. It was scary how my mind refused to let my body move. It wasn't until I sur-rendered any hope of living without her that I could physi-cally move again. I was deeply depressed, edging closer to feeling totally out of control.

As my sister observed my depressive state, she tried her best to help. She knew that I was a reader, so she started giving me any Christian self-help books she had. As I read one after another, they only made my problems worse. The books could in some way tell me what might be wrong with me, but they seemed to have no solutions. I was looking for something wrong with me that I could fix, because I still didn't understand grief. Grief was the problem, but I had no idea it could be so debilitating. I never knew anyone who had suffered this kind of pain. I felt guilty and ashamed that I felt so bad over someone who didn't love me and had left me. I thought I should just get up and move on—happy to be free from a bad marriage.

I suspect that, to some extent, Annie was my idol and that I, at some level, was codependent. However, there were bigger factors at work. Our marriage was a dismal failure from the first night; but over time, God's grace in answer to my prayers made Annie the love of my life. Somehow ripping apart our relationship was an attack on my relationship with our Father. Furthermore, we had spent twenty years in the fundamentalist cult. To have worked our way through the cult and finally escaped had brought us closer together than two buddies on a battlefield—at least from my perspective. I thought we were comrades in arms for life, and I didn't think anything or anyone could separate us after that. So this was a betrayal so huge that I couldn't wrap my mind around it. If only she had stabbed me to death. Then I could have uttered, "Et tu, Brute," and died in her arms. Instead, I was a rat caught in the inescapable and interminable maze of my own mind. I could never find an answer that would stick.

My days became bleaker and bleaker, and my efforts to find answers were falling flat. Where books by Charles Stanley had been enjoyable in the past, they now seemed like sawdust to my soul. Some old tapes from the Dallas pastor provided a little purpose, but circumstances in his past had made his ministry suspect. I wondered if I should be listening to him. As I perused the books Patricia gave me, the thought of seeking counseling once again challenged me. I still had in the back of my mind the notion that God might not look kindly on counseling; but I had to take that chance. I had to settle on something or I was likely to go insane. I decided to limit my input to Bible reading, listening to the Dallas pastor, and going to counseling. I would pursue this course in an effort to determine whether there was any hope. If that didn't work, I figured it was the end of the line.

While reading Patricia's self-help books, I came across a reference to a Christian counseling organization. They had offices about twenty miles away. I solicited the help of my sister Elaine to chauffer me to the counseling sessions because, by this time, I felt so emotionally unstable that I didn't think I could navigate the Chicago-area traffic fifty minutes back and forth. As we traveled the local freeways, I stared out the window like a mesmerized child. I watched as the wheels on the big trucks went round and round. I looked at the sides of their trailers to see the company logos and the advertising. One day I saw one that had G. O. D. in big red letters; then, in smaller letters: 1-800-CALL-GOD.

But I sure wasn't getting any answers. It was as if God never answered when I called. Nothing made sense any- more. Why did anyone get up in the morning and go to work. It just ended each day only to start again. Same ol', same ol'—people caught on a treadmill, going nowhere. When they fell off, someone would bury them. I prayed that God would have someone bury me!

At first the Christian counseling went nowhere. Cal was a fine Christian man, about my age, and a former pastor in addition to being an adept counselor. When I began my ses- sions with him, I looked for sins in my life that would explain why God would allow me to suffer like this. Cal would listen and smile gently. He tried to convince me that my sins were minor league. He thought my problem was simply grief. Well, what the heck! Now what? I still didn't get it. If it was "just grief," I figured there was nothing wrong with me. I should be able to jump up and get on with life. What was my problem? I returned home as confused and as anxious as ever. It seemed like counseling was another bust.

My last glimmers of hope were fading fast, and I continued to ask God to take me home. I had no reason to live. There was no way life would ever be worth living again. Even if Annie were to change her mind and call to tell me that she was the one who had been at fault, it wouldn't have mattered. I had been totally undone. I suspect I was suffering posttraumatic stress disorder. I was Humpty-Dumpty: I had fallen off the ledge—or gone over the edge—and was irreparably broken. There was no putting me back together again. I needed to die.

I remembered reading that Billy Graham once said that he had never contemplated suicide, but that he had been in so much pain that he didn't want to go on living. He had asked the Lord to take him home. By comparison to such an honorable man, I felt dishonorable. I was in so much pain that not only did I not *want* to go on; I didn't think that I *could* go on. If you can't go on and the Lord won't take you, what are your options? In the evangelical environment of Christianity where smiles on Sunday morning seem to come easy for most, and life looks upward and mobile, the suggestion of a Christian committing suicide is reprehensible. I felt as though I was rapidly approaching the end. I didn't know how much longer I could hang on.

Looking back on those days when the end seemed near, I know now that it was the God of Isaiah holding me together. It did not feel like it then, but the God who regards upholding the universe as a drop in the bucket was holding me. Humpty-Dumpty is not a problem for the God of the heavens!

CHAPTER 15
A RING OF FIRE

For we do not want you to be ignorant brethren, of our trouble which came to us in Asia: that we were burdened beyond measure, above strength, so that we despaired even of life. Yes, we had the sentence of death in ourselves.
—2 Corinthians 1:8-9

New Year's had come and gone. My sister and I had retrieved all my earthly belongings from my college apartment on the Saturday after Thanksgiving. I felt obligated to pay my year's worth of rent if necessary, but I didn't want to fight to get my property. I was afraid that the landlord might do something with my thousands of dollars' worth of books. Annie and I had split up our belongings, and I was left with about $30,000 worth of possessions. Even though they just about fit into one room, they were valuable to me. And now I could sleep in my own bed.

Then came a cold morning in late January. My sister had left for work, and the mid-morning sky was gray and overcast. Sitting on the sofa reading the Bible, I was trying to gain enough stability to make breakfast. Suddenly the acrid smell of smoke pierced my nostrils. My eyes quickly scanned the room and saw nothing out of the ordinary. I got up to search the kitchen and found no hint of smoke. I wondered if the garbage chute was on fire. I unlocked the door and stepped out into the hallway. There was smoke in the air and smoke coming from the holes around the light fixture by the elevator. I could hear conversation from an adjacent hallway. I heard voices and knocking on doors.

I scurried inside and got dressed for winter in Chicago. I went over to the patio window and saw smoke coming out from between the top of the wall and the roof. It turned out that the area above our ceiling and inside the roof was beginning to light up like an old Christmas tree. I gathered what few things I couldn't live without and walked to the door. By this time the smoke was thicker and the voices and noises in the hallway louder. People who lived on the upper floors were evacuating down the interior stairway, since the elevator would be a short ride to death. Quickly, I was out the door, and holding an extra winter coat and an extra pair of pants, I watched the fire increase. As I retreated from the building, the first fire truck arrived.

By now the flames were bursting forth from various areas of the large apartment building. Several more fire trucks arrived from Palatine and adjacent municipalities. The fire raged. I stood, dumbfounded, in one of the vast parking lots of the enormous apartment complex. My sister's apartment was on an upper floor, and I watched as the firemen broke out my bedroom window and tossed my flaming king-size mattress over the side and to the ground. It all seemed surreal; and, since Annie no longer occupied the bed with me, it didn't seem to matter. Our bed, like our marriage, had now gone up in smoke.

The loss of all my earthly possessions was infinitesimal compared to the loss of Annie, my business, and my home. It did afford some cover for my real pain. Others could certainly acknowledge physical loss. It was something tangible that I could hide behind for a few days. My sister soon rented another apartment, and it was to some extent an improvement. I had tried to cry a few times at her previous place, though it was totally foreign and offensive to my manhood. The tears could get no traction. I once popped my head outside the apartment door just as the next-door neighbor had done likewise. He kind of stared at me as if to say, "Are you the big baby I hear crying in the bedroom next to mine?" I couldn't cry another tear there.

My state of mind had grown progressively worse. The apartment complex was a concrete and asphalt jungle. I would go out for a walk and encounter desperate-looking women smoking outside their apartment. I wondered whether I would end up smoking again in an attempt to dull the pain, or whether I would get sexually desperate enough to follow this woman into her reeking bed? Will I become homeless because I am even too nuts for my sister to have around? Oh God, please kill me right on this very spot! Please, please, please!

I never knew I could hurt this bad—and still be alive. I never knew! Oh Lord, let me die! I don't know what to think. I don't know what to do. Let me die, Lord, let me die. I don't want to die. Lord, heal me, Lord, help! I still didn't know what had hit me. I wished it had been a Mack truck. Father, why did you let this happen? What now, why now? Don't you love me? Don't you care about me? Why Father, why, why, why? Please, dear God, please! This isn't what I expected.

As Patricia and I moved into the new apartment, there was nothing to be moved. Everything had to be bought or rented. I soon had a new bed and some plastic slide-open containers that served as a dresser and a nightstand. I still had content coverage with Annie on our household belongings; however, it would only cover 5 percent of our policy outside of our house. This gave me about $5500 coverage instead of the approximately $30,000 I needed. I had money in the bank, but at this rate it would soon be gone. After Patricia settled with her insurance company, she insisted on giving me several thousand dollars. She saw how everything was a psychological struggle, and she was trying to diminish any extra pressure.

The days continued to drag on in anxiety, fear, and pain. I still felt guilty for being physically healthy but emotionally debilitated. I was ashamed of what I later discovered was grief. I felt like my whole Christian walk had been down a wrong path without even knowing it. What was real and what was false?

One morning as I sat pondering what to do next, I opened my Bible to the first chapter of 2 Corinthians. We had covered all the epistles of Paul nine ways to Sunday during the twenty years in the cult. I once had stacks of notebooks on all of them that, when torched, would keep a small village warm for the winter. "Grace to you and peace from God our Father and the Lord Jesus Christ" had been parsed with a microscope. But now something jumped from the page into my eye sockets. I got past the greeting and the words of comfort that I was not experiencing to verse eight. Paul wrote to his audience that he did not want them ignorant of his trouble in Asia. Then he wrote: "… we were burdened beyond measure above strength, so that we *despaired, even of life*." What? Paul went on and declared: "Yes, we had the sentence of death in ourselves." Wow! Unbelievable. This was Paul, the great Paul?! We had been taught that Paul made something like one mistake in his thirty years of ministry. Strong, tough, righteous, a no-nonsense, suck-you-up and spit-you-out Christian. Not a weak, impetuous wimp like Peter or a mama's boy like Timothy. The word "despair" means 'to be at a loss psychologically, be in great difficulty, doubt, embarrassment (in reference here to living)." Paul, in the will of God, was saying that he did not know how to go on living. Whatever the circumstance that brought about Paul's mindset, he was whipped. In the plan of God and despairing, even of life! I took a deep breath and let out a long sigh for the first time in nine months. Maybe I wasn't crazy. Maybe I wasn't dishonorable. The supposedly roughest, toughest, most successful Christian ever was in the plan of God and despairing of life just like weak old me. Hallelujah, thank you Lord! Later I would investigate why God would allow such suffering in his plan; but for now, I was just glad to be sane.

CHAPTER 16
WISHFUL THINKING

Because the Lord has been witness between you and the wife of your youth, with whom you have dealt treacherously; yet she is your companion and wife by covenant.
—Malachi 2:14

"For the Lord God of Israel says that he hates divorce, for it covers one's garment with violence," says the Lord of Hosts. Therefore, take heed to your spirit that you do not deal treacherously."
—Malachi 2: 16

Although I was free to come and go to and from the apartment as I pleased, I felt like I was a POW. I had no emotional stability and was afraid to venture very far from the apartment. Each encounter with another human being was embarrassing. I thought that my searing, screaming pain was written all over my face and demeanor. But life in the new apartment gave a glimmer of light. The buildings were newer and had a fresher feel. The sidewalks allowed for extensive walking without commercial traffic whizzing by at highway speeds. More windows allowed the sunshine to brighten the environment. As early spring arrived, the chirping birds in the budding trees outside the kitchen window helped take an edge off my continuing darkness and pain.

As my outlook began to brighten ever so slightly and slowly, I purchased my first computer and got hooked up to the internet. I soon ran into online bridge games that allowed me to play with real people in real time. I wanted human contact but at no risk of revealing who I was or what my situation was. I had learned how to play bridge as a teenager, but I had had no real opportunities to play in the last twenty-five years. Now I had the chance to play when I wanted to. I discovered that bridge was the only thing that—when I was fully concentrating on it—could drown out my life and my pain. It was my first activity beyond restless sleep that gave me some respite from my overanxious thoughts. I could chat with my bridge partner and our opponents. They couldn't see me, and we would never meet. This was a good thing.

Then one day, Annie called. She said that she wanted to drive up and see me. Hope was alive! Maybe happy times were just around the corner. A few adjustments to our life in the Lord, and we could get on with a new exciting life together. I asked her to bring our youngest German shepherd puppy along with her, and she agreed to. Together again!

We agreed on a day and time and set it for a few days later, and, after negotiating the madness known as Chicago traffic, Annie arrived. My optimism was short-lived. I opened the door and greeted her with the hope of an embrace. It had been nearly eight months since I had last seen her and a year and a half since she had let me hold her. But no affection was forthcoming. Her greeting was very cool. I beckoned her to come in, offered her a seat in an easy chair and a glass of tea. She accepted both and began her search for words. When she found them, they were short and to the point. She said that, upon our separation, she missed my physical presence and realized that some sort of love existed toward me over the course of the last eighteen years. However, she soon got over my absence and decided that she would rather spend the rest of her life alone than with someone she never truly loved.

She declared that she really didn't have anything more to say, that she had simply wanted to tell me in person rather than over the phone. She suggested that I take Eli for a walk, and then she would be on her way. Eighteen years of marriage, six years of premarital interest, and a year of waiting on pins and needles, all gone in ninety seconds. It was quick, quiet, and violent! Stupefied, I went to our van, got the young dog out of his crate, and took him on the most uninspired walk of his life. I don't think I could have hurt any worse if Muhammad Ali had pummeled me for ninety seconds.

Annie had spoken. It was over. No solutions were forthcoming. My mind acknowledged the finality, and my soul staggered. My body wanted no part of me. It was sick of carrying my soul's pain.

⌐ • ⌐

While my sister had been looking for a permanent residence, I had decided to double up on my counseling sessions. By my standards, counseling was expensive, but it seemed to be the only place I could even begin to relax. Cal was the only person I could talk with and feel like his words were more than opinion. One fifty-minute session was not enough to relieve my anxiety; I would leave not much better than I was when I arrived. Doubling up my sessions allowed me to think through what was on my mind and listen to what Cal was saying. Finally, I was relaxed enough that I could eat the one meal of the week that would not stick in my throat and that my stomach would not repel. I would drive from Cal's office to the nearest McDonald's and tell them to "super-size it." The double quarter-pounder with cheese, large fries, and unlimited Coke may have been clogging my arteries, but I could sit there in relative obscurity and let the food slide down my esophagus without feeling that I was choking to death.

Cal soon became aware of my two obsessions: Annie and the Bible. I had studied the Bible vigorously for the last thirty years. All of Cal's counsel would have to be biblically based for me to be satisfied with it. Worldly solutions and Christian platitudes wouldn't work with me. If the advice was not something that lined up with the Word of God, my soul would not accept it. Cal realized this, and he enjoyed our in-depth biblical conversations.

And then the simplicity of pure genius happened! I believe that Holy Spirit took over. Perhaps it was simply Cal's wonderful wisdom, but it was the first effective breakthrough in my soul. After nine months of clinging to life by my fingernails, I received my first real glimpse of hope.

Trena Leep's boys don't cry; neither do her girls, for that matter! When my mother was just four, her mother died in the flu pandemic. Three of my mother's sisters—each of them named Gertrude—died before they reached school age. She was left with a father who few could remember ever smiling, a much older sister, and seven brothers. There was no place for weakness in this hardscrabble existence— and no time for tears. My mother passed these traits on to her children. Obviously, a parent should not indulge frequent tears of complaint and whining; but we never even learned to acknowledge any legitimate pain. By denying my pain, I carried a lifetime of baggage.

Cal turned toward me, holding an empty coffee cup. As he slowly turned his cup upside down, he asked, "What am I doing?"

"Theoretically, you are spilling your coffee on the floor," I replied.

"How did I do that?" he countered.

"You poured it out," I said.

Cal smiled and said, "You're absolutely correct: I poured out my coffee all over the floor! Now look at what King David says in the Psalms." Turning to Psalm 142, Cal read the first couple of verses: "I pour out my complaint before Him, I declare before Him my trouble. When my spirit was overwhelmed within me, then you knew my path." Cal continued in Psalm 62:8, where David says to pour out your heart before Him.

"Look here at Psalm 6, verses six and seven," Cal said. "David says he is weary of his groaning and that his bed is a waterbed of tears. All night he cries. His eyes waste away from grief."

I think I may have stopped breathing. I looked at Cal with a blank stare. My first thought must have been one of incredulity. I stammered to speak, but my mind was fractured. My thoughts lay in pieces. I had heard a pastor once mention David making his bed a waterbed of tears, but it was the wrong person at the wrong time. Now Cal, a strong and gentle man, was leading me to still waters.

Cal continued: "You can pour anything out before the Lord. He is a God big enough to handle it. Scream, shout, cry, complain—he is there with you." I knew it was true. These were the first words of real comfort to impact my soul. God knows his children. He knew I grew up without permission to cry. He knew I spent twenty more years in a tearless cult. But he also knew the cult regarded King David as the Badass of the Bible. He was a man's man. He brought King Saul two hundred foreskins to acquire his wife. He could kill at the drop of a hat. He was a confessed adulterer and murderer. Yet he was a man after God's own heart. Bad to the bone—but cry like a baby? No, he cried like a man!

At that moment, I had no idea of the ramifications of our conversation, but I was convinced of one thing: I could cry and I would still be a man. This was the most incredible breakthrough of our counseling sessions. It countered everything I had known. It countered my "Christian upbringing," it countered my Christian adulthood, and it countered our baggage-carrying, pain-hiding culture. Here is the archetypal man, a man after God's own heart, pouring out his heart to God and crying like a water faucet on his bed in the night. For me, crying would have been comparable to wetting my bed. I may have cried on one or two occasions, but the pain was then only superseded by the shame.

Permission to cry brought my soul its first wave of relief. Philosophically, it validated my pain. Psychologically, I discovered that unbridled tears relieved the physical anxiety that, during my life, had made certain circumstances almost unbearable. In these grief-worn days it began to diminish the constant pain-anxiety mixture that made suicide look like the only relief.

Slowly, each morning as I sat before the Lord, I would let the tears flow as I held the Bible in my hands. As the Lord broke down my inhibitions, they rolled. From the time I would reluctantly get up with an aching head until two hours later, they would roll. I would find myself on my knees as close to the floor as possible. It seemed as though there was no air to breathe more than an inch off the floor.

Early on I didn't say much, but as the days turned into weeks and the weeks into months, I finally could tell the Lord that losing Annie hurt. Most of my life I had spent knowing that God knew everything, so it didn't seem to make much sense to tell him anything. That was so crazy. Here was the beginning of a walking, talking relationship with my Abba. In the meantime, I would get up off the floor after a couple of hours of tears, and my overnight headaches would be gone. Although I was still deep in the forest of grief, the Lord was shining a ray of hope in on my dark circumstances. I had no clue about the way out, but tears were the best medicine for the anxiety and pain that I could have ever hoped for. I had never known how similar fear and anxiety felt. Tears relieved my anxiety—and with it the fearful feeling of being out of control. The tears gave me my first opportunity for clear-headed thinking in almost a year. And much to my surprise, I was meeting two new friends, David and God!

CHAPTER 17
SOUL FOOD

The Lord God has given me the tongue of the learned, that I should know how to speak a word in season to him who is weary. He awakens me morning by morning, He awakens my ear to hear as the learned. The Lord has opened my ear and I was not rebellious, nor did I turn away.
—Isaiah 50:4–5

Answer me speedily, O Lord; my spirit fails. Do not hide your face from me, lest I be like those who go down into the pit. Cause me to hear your lovingkindness in the morning, for in you do I trust; cause me to know the way in which I should walk, for I lift up my soul to you.
—Psalm 143:7–8.

T ears were good, but they were not a magic bullet. Crying was a valve that released the pressure of all my anxieties and unanswered thoughts, but I was still caught in a hopeless maze. Each morning brought nothing new. I wasn't in any mood to sing "Great is Thy Faithfulness" because I was not seeing new mercies. Each new morning brought the same old dismal, painful reality: Annie was gone, my business was gone, my house was gone, my dogs were gone—everything I cherished was gone. And having it all back would no longer be the answer. I couldn't see the future for the pain. I couldn't imagine ever being able to love again. I couldn't imagine ever being sane again.

It was becoming clear that my situation was about more than my losses. The Lord was up to something, and he was changing my soul forever. If Annie were to suddenly choose reconciliation, I had traveled too far to pick up anywhere close to where we left off. My brokenness left me incapable; my time with the Lord left Annie and me incompatible. A future either with or without her offered little hope.

After a double session with Cal and the "happy meal" at McDonalds that I had anticipated for a week, I started making a new detour on my way home. I was at the peak of my week in terms of stability, and I wanted to take full advantage of it. No, it was not going to be a bar or a brothel that would bring me hope, but rather a bookstore—a large Christian bookstore, to be exact. I would be calm enough to peruse the bookshelves at length, looking for any Christian wisdom regarding my pain. God wasn't stuffing my mailbox with books on pain, grief, and suffering; it's noteworthy that there never was much available on the subject. A book would not appear until after the Lord had shown me the same principles in his word. It seemed that he was going to personally comfort me before he let someone else share his words with me.

As I looked high and low, I reexamined some of the authors I had lost in the fire at my sister's apartment. Brennan Manning had continued to publish, and his new books seemed to be even kinder and gentler. Andrew Murray, the one shining star from my Dutch Reformed background (whom I had never heard of while in the Christian Reformed Church) continued to bless me with his benevolent view of God. I soon discovered George MacDonald, and what a happy meal he became, as he delivered a revealing picture

of a most magnificent and beautiful God that only his difficult words could capture.

Each week, instead of finding a book that spoke directly
to my immediate need, I would reluctantly leave the bookstore carrying with me something that spoke about God, but
did not speak to my pain. I remained under the Lord's house
arrest. He was a benevolent jailer, but I felt imprisoned just
the same. I might venture a few blocks down the street to
shoot hoops, attempting a skill that I had never developed.
I might rush out for a walk of a mile or two, but would
hurry back home to get before the Lord—lest my anxiety
overwhelm me. Each day I would do as many pushups and
abdominal crunches as I could. I was trying to tire myself
out so as to get some nightmare-free sleep, and also to try
to maintain some physical health in case I were to survive.
It scared me to think I might never be stable enough to work
again. I wondered what gutter I would live in when my
money ran out. Each morning my efforts were focused on
trying to get on with life, but each new day brought another
failed day. At least that's the way it seemed to me.

If you were to ask the Lord for his perspective, I think
he would tell you he had the situation well in hand. Yes,
he was showing me new mercies day by day: they were
days he made, and he was making them for me, too! I was
just too drunk with pain to know, and I think that is how
he wanted it. He had my full attention, and he was going
to take his time. I was God's new creation in Christ Jesus,
and I had told him, "Whatever it takes." Okay then. No, it
wasn't okay—it wasn't okay by a long shot!

CHAPTER 18
A JUGGLING ACT

Unless the Lord had been my help, my soul soon would have settled in silence. In the multitude of anxieties within me, your comforts delight my soul.
—Psalm 94:17, 19

Narrow is the gate and difficult is the way which leads to life and there are few that find it.
—Matthew 7:14

Come unto me all you who are heavy laden and I will give you rest. Take my yoke upon you and learn from me, for I am gentle and lowly in heart, and you will find rest for your souls. For my yoke is easy and my burden is light.
—Matthew 11:28–30

Watching a juggling act late one night on a fifty-year-old episode of the Ed Sullivan Show made me think of its many parallels to life. Fresh out of the womb, about the only ball in the air seems to be the physical life God gave us. We are grateful as God adds various balls, oranges, or bowling pins to our lives, be it a job, spouse, children, grandchildren, good health, and so forth. As we share a balancing act with him in his marvelous provision of grace toward us, life is good or, at the very least, hopeful. But suddenly, if we drop a ball, or when other people or

99

circumstances, or even the sovereign God, intervene, we are thrown off-balance as we try to keep everything else in rhythm. The worse-case scenario: we end up with five or six bowling pins in our arms that eventually drop to the floor.

Losing Annie was catastrophic; everything else paled in comparison. And when everything else was added to that, it was off the charts. I had run across a study online that evaluated life-change and the impact it had on a person. There were numbers assigned to each kind of change, be it divorce, job loss, relocation, burnt-down house, death of a loved one, and so on. They assigned different levels of danger that these changes caused. I remember that a score of 300-350 put your life at high risk: you were in need of some serious professional help and observation. When I added up the numbers they assigned to my major issues, the score came to an astronomical 1125.

The greatest loss (after the loss of Annie) was my inability to work and the sale of our business. Since I was five or six years old, work in the real world had been the best outlet for my introverted personality — and my greatest form of recreation. My parents had a small dairy (convenience) store that gave me the opportunity to candle eggs, sweep floors, dust shelves, sort pop bottles, stock milk and candy, and wait on customers at an early age. I was using an adding machine and a cash register when I was only a first-grader. Best of all, I got to hang out with my older siblings.

They say that a man's work is often what he lets define him. I wasn't necessarily defined by my work (most people might suggest that I was a biblical nut-job), but it sure was a lot of fun. I ran into the game of Risk in our pastor's basement when I was a teenager. I soon figured out a winning strategy that, decades later, I transferred to the sandwich business. I had worked for nine years and for two owners in that business by the time Randy and I ventured into business for ourselves. I wasn't going into business to feel like a bigshot. I was simply trying to have fun and make up for the time I lost in the cult, a time in which our finances never got off the ground.

The business fit my personality makeup beautifully. My route truck was my office, where I could figure out all the problems that needed solving (I had filled the need for another employee by doubling as a route salesman myself). This gave me the opportunity to play the game of Risk at the street level. I was good at it. What Randy and I had mostly consolidated in our nine years of employment under other owners, we conquered when we were turned loose on the market as owners. With quality control of our product and energized service and merchandizing, we soon doubled, tripled, and quadrupled our customer sales. To say that they were happy is an understatement. We seldom lost a customer. I actually gave up some accounts to our competition—what little remained of it—in order to have time for bigger accounts that were looking for us.

With no wife, no business, and no children to focus on, with my relaxing home life gone, and wondering what I had done to deserve this kind of treatment from God, I felt like I had been knocked down by a welter of the aforementioned oranges, balls, and bowling pins. But God had been in my corner from the get-go, though it was unbeknownst to me. He had a greater prosperity in mind. Men in general—and me in particular—are often inclined more toward mental input than output. Unlike women, who usually have a much greater and closer support group, men rarely talk about their problems with their male friends or relatives. They just keep working them over in their heads.

Science has recently discovered a reality that God has built into our minds and souls. We need to talk to someone in order to get at the crux of our problems. Men can try to solve their problems and others' problems by telling someone what to do (with little success), whereas women can talk about their problems without giving each other solutions; then those seeking a solution come up with their own solution. The apparent reason for this success is that, when we talk about a problem, we transfer it from one side of the brain (where we can't make any headway) to the other side of the brain (where we can solve our own problem). This explains why prayer can be of great benefit to anyone who thinks he is talking to God. By mentioning our problems to God, we have just transferred our problem to the side of the brain that can deal with it. It explains why anyone, even an atheist, could probably report some benefit from prayer.

My counselor Cal may or may not have been aware of these specifics when he suggested that I start journaling. This was his recommendation: "Address any issues you might have with someone on paper and assume they would read it. Instead of sending it, just file it until further needed." My "issue list" was short, and I soon found myself journaling my conversations with God. Instead of just reading the Bible and stuffing my mind with information, I would journal on any subject that piqued my interest. Then the dance would begin. I would set down my pen and ask a question, and the answer would pop into my head before I finished the question. It was fascinating: God was playing with me, and after a while I realized he was having fun, too. Even as I sat in a heap of bowling pins and oranges, God was quietly rebuilding my life from the ground up. An infrastructure of emotional stability was being constructed, even though I was still a nervous wreck.

CHAPTER 19
THAT'S WHAT FRIENDS ARE FOR

Save me, O God! For the waters have come up to my neck. I sink in deep mire, where there is no standing.
—Psalm 69:1

Reproach has broken my heart, and I am full of heaviness; I looked for someone to take pity, but there was none.
—Psalm 69:20

Sometimes friends destroy each other, but there is a friend who sticks closer than a brother.
—Proverbs 18:24 (expanded alternative translation)

In my effort to get on with life, I thought maybe I could start to reach out to my friends and acquaintances. Maybe one of them could offer me some wisdom or solace, something that would encourage me to reach outside myself and to start living. None were within visiting distance in my condition, but maybe email would be a vehicle for comfort. I launched my first missive, and it apparently missed its intended target. Whatever I said with regard to my situation inspired this reply: "We either get better or we get bitter." Granted, the man was not my bosom buddy, but he had been close enough to help me during a desperate moment in my business life. I thought that he might understand my great loss because he had lost his first wife to cancer; but he certainly misinterpreted my pain.

Bitterness was the farthest thing from my thoughts. One of my big problems was that I had compassion for Annie's situation. I felt bad that she had married me under duress from the pulpit. I felt terrible that she was caught in a marriage that was involuntary. I sided with her against myself. On one hand, I was madly in love with her; on the other, I felt that the whole marriage was a sham—and I was taking the blame for it on myself. My sisters reminded me that my wife was twenty-five when she said "I do," and no one was holding a gun to her head. But no one could really understand the effect the cult mentality had on our volition. So, once again, there was no one to truly share my predicament with.

I soon discovered that, no matter how much someone may love you, there are few who can handle anything beyond some short-term pain. They instinctively want to fix you before your pain rubs off on them. When their platitudes and normal kindnesses fail to heal, they turn and walk away, disappointed that you didn't get with the program.

Maybe I could creep back to church, sneak into a back row, and go unmolested as I tried to enjoy singing—something I had dearly missed. It was a crazy thing. In the cult, singing was dismissed as insignificant. Most old-time hymns were made fun of because they were supposedly inaccurate as a literal doctrinal statement from the Bible. It was as if no allowances were made for the fact that God used poetry and all kinds of nonliteral means in the Bible to convey truth. Happily, distanced from that environment for almost ten years, I had come to see how much freedom God has given us in our expression of worship through music. In reading the Psalms and being admonished to make a loud noise to the Lord, I became aware that there was room for even the most raucous vibes. I loved it. I was a middle-aged fan of the rock-and-roll of the 1960s and 1970s, and the modern Christian music scene was certainly music to my ears! My first real exposure to the upbeat music I loved came in a Vineyard church that I had attended during the last year I had spent with Annie. Although by this time she had refused to attend church with me (she accompanied me once and liked the pastor's message but did not want to make a commitment to anything that would have any emotional connection with me), I did find great purpose in my own attendance. Ironically, it was the music that spoke to my soul as much as did the messages, which were good.

After Annie left me, the pain was too great to carry into church with the "happy Sunday morning crowd." But I was always pushing myself, thinking that this was the way to get better. Thus I attended church one Sunday, hoping to hide in my anonymity. Church had barely begun—one song in—when we were told to turn and greet someone near us. Oh crap! No! I greeted a man older than me, hoping that we could leave it at that; but no, he was going to go the extra mile. I tried to beat around the bush, but the barrage of questions seemed like torture: "Where do you live? Where do you work? Are you married?" I couldn't figure out a nice way to tell him that this was painful and also none of his business, so I told him a little of my story. He looked at me as though I were some curiosity and then slowly turned away. I felt like I had leprosy. As soon as the service was over, I scurried back to my sister's condo, feeling like a cornered mouse.

The next morning, as I contemplated how I might reboot my church-going efforts, a dear friend called me. Dave had been a part of our inner sanctum. In church, in choir, in our dynamic conversations after church, in our small group, Dave was a sure and true presence. He had left our Baptist church for a different church in Indianapolis, and had soon found himself in love and, not long afterwards, married. He knew of my calamity, but he was 175 miles away and dealing with all the newness of marriage. In the providence of God, he felt led to return to school. Dave was interested in Trinity International University in Deerfield, Illinois, particularly their cohort-based adult education. He called to see if I would like to accompany him on a campus visit to check out the program. I felt too unsteady to think about returning to school myself. I didn't feel that I could even spend ten minutes talking to anyone on campus, let alone go back to classes. But as gentle and quiet as Dave is, he encouraged me to join him. Since he promised to pick me up and take me back home, combined with the fact I lived less than twenty miles from the campus, I reluctantly agreed.

I followed Dave around campus like a little puppy, though I felt like an old arthritic dog. My emotions were still so full of pain and instability that it was hard to traverse the campus and stand like a statue as we interacted with recruitment and enrollment personnel. Somehow, Bob, the recruiter, was able to extract enough information from me to assure me he would pray for my flat-lining marriage, and he convinced me to go through the enrollment procedure. Quite the salesman!

As Dave drove me home, he told me that he had decided that he could not afford the cost of a move from economical central Indiana to the high-rent district of the Chicago suburbs. My acceptance to Trinity's cohort program arrived in the mail shortly thereafter. The Lord had used a dear friend to gently push me out of my asylum into a classroom environment that he had perfectly tailored for me.

Shortly after Dave returned to Indiana, the divorce papers arrived: Final dissolution. The state treated our marriage like a bad stain. Dissolved, like it never happened. While this appears to be the view of marriage and divorce in the new millennium, I knew God took a different view. I had prayed until my heart was empty and my brain was dry. I prayed until my body ached and my head hurt. I prayed, prayed, prayed—prayed for twenty-two months. I got squat.

God hates divorce! God is absolutely for marriage! He was in covenant with us, and he could make this happen. Why was he walking away? He is the all-things-are-possible God. I had pestered him for twenty-two months—just as he instructed. I knew that he could have looked down the corridors of time and made sure Annie would have been a woman who responded positively in the end, or could have arranged my life in such a way that I would have married a different woman who would have responded positively. I knew he wanted us to stay married or, once we had split up, to reconcile. Dissolution, never! Twenty-five years of memories don't dissolve. But there was no solution to the dissolution. And there were no solutions forthcoming for my war-torn soul.

Reconciliation? Not likely. It took Annie eighteen years to decide to divorce me. A very private person, she would find being alone more to her liking. Tottering up to me when we would be in our nineties, saying that she had changed her mind, was not desirable. My convictions before the Lord required me to wait. My state of emotions and mind didn't leave me in a place to go wife-shopping, and the responsibility toward reconciliation only compounded my angst. Well then, it was just God and me. Hmm? Not being quick on the uptake, I didn't register this. I kept praying for reconciliation, without any realistic expectation of it. The struggle to live continued.

⌐ • ⌐

After a rain-drenched night, I dribbled my basketball down the sidewalk as I ambled toward a court close to the condo. I grabbed the ball and stopped in my tracks. I bent to get a closer look at a long, sticky worm. I sat on my haunches, quietly observing. I reached down and placed him in the grass. He wasn't sticky. Washed clean, he could get no traction. With the clouds receding, his future would have been worm jerky.

I reached the park and fired some potshots at the basket. Clang, clang, clang—until I finally reverted to the skyhook I had developed in the league of forty-year-olds—doctors, lawyers, and CEOs—that I had played in some years earlier. Sucking for air, I stood up as the bright sun warmed me in the cool breeze. In an unusually quiet moment, there was momentary peace in my weary soul. Courted by the Lord, but without a clue.

Back in my study, with my Bible open, I listened as he sang the Psalms to me. Bold in his exclusive love, he showed off. Love was throbbing in my heart, and he left me awestruck and undone. He unleashed the hounds of heaven, and his mercy and unfailing love tackled me. He was playing hard. I hadn't got squat? No, not squat, but a dynamic answer to a different conversation. I looked for God in every crack and crevice. Maybe the worm didn't talk, but he was more than just a donkey.

CHAPTER 20
FIVE-FOOT-FOUR AND SO MUCH MORE

And rejoice with the wife of your youth. As a loving deer and a graceful doe, let her breasts satisfy you at all times.
—Proverbs 5:18b–19a.

Now there was leaning on Jesus' bosom one of his disciples, whom Jesus loved. Then leaning back on Jesus' breast, he said to him....
—John 13:23, 25a.

On a lazy Saturday morning, I meandered up to the registration table. After a quick query, the woman in charge pointed to the paperwork I needed to fill out. I picked up the packet and scanned the top page. As I turned and raised my head, I was struck head-on by a Valley-girl greeting. Freckle-faced, with a wall-to-wall smile, covered in a cape and beret, she launched her face into my personal space, and greeted me:

"Hi!" It was so effusive, it was abusive.

"Hi," I replied, startled.

"I'm Lynn!" she exclaimed.

"I'm Garry," I replied. She then started peppering me with questions, and soon my worst fears were realized: we were going to be classmates, not for just one course, but for the whole twenty-one-month cohort of classes on communications. Oh my, what hath God wrought!

Monday evening came, and I found my way into a comfortable classroom with tables configured in a large U-shape, with four or five large executive chairs parked behind each side of the U. Fortunately, I was on the front side of the U, and Lynn was on the back, safely some thirty feet away. The four-hour class was soon over, and I beat a path back home.

The next Monday I arrived to find that the seats on my side of the U were taken. I glanced around the room: the bottom side of the U was empty, as were most of the backside seats. Ms. Ditz had not yet arrived, so I avoided her side of the room and sat on the bottom. As the rest of our cohort slowly arrived, they claimed every seat except the one adjacent to me on my left. Lynn finally appeared, and with only one choice, sat down next to me—as she gave me a whimsical look.

Lynn's sitting next to me was a distraction but, I must admit, not such an unpleasant one. I was still deeply depressed, my sex drive exceedingly suppressed, my life a distressed mess, but I was not yet dead. I didn't view Lynn as dating material: first, I was committed to the Lord if he wanted me to reconcile with my ex-wife; furthermore, I soon noticed a big rock on Lynn's left ring finger. Where I came from, that rendered her off-limits. But she was an all-American woman with a country-and-western figure, evoking the song lyrics, "If I told you, you have a beautiful body, would you hold it against me?"

Our communications prof divided the class into three groups. The scenario was this: We were all survivors of a plane crash in the desert, and with a flashlight, a loaded revolver, adequate clothing, and little or no food and water.

What would we as a group do — stay with the plane or walk for help? We all either had to stay or go. In addition to me, our group consisted of Lynn, another young woman, a young man, and former Chicago Bears wide receiver Anthony Morgan. Morgan, recently retired, was young and in world-class shape.

On our initial vote, Anthony and I wanted to walk, while Lynn and the others wanted to stay. After intense debate and persuasion, we convinced the young man to walk. Lynn was irate, but the majority ruled. The prof soon called the class to order and declared our fate: Those who had stayed with the plane lived; those who had walked died. I thought I would never hear the end of it from Lynn. I was a pure knucklehead. But by the time we ate supper together, she was laughing, saying that the next time she would use the gun to shoot me so that everybody else would have to stay with the plane. We were fast becoming friends. I had a dynamo on my hands, not a ditz.

The next week I brought supper for the class, and Lynn and I sat side by side. At the end of the evening, Lynn asked me if I needed help carrying cooking gear to my truck. We packed the gear in the back and blabbed on about the night's activities. As she signaled her departure, Lynn quietly gathered me into a gentle embrace. I think she said good night, but I'm not sure. I couldn't hear, I could only feel!

Hugs and kisses were not part of my culture or upbringing. Only spouses were exempt from a hands-off policy, and there certainly were no public displays of affection. I had held and hugged Annie daily for much of our marriage, expressing my love toward her, nuanced in a million ways. When Lynn hugged me, time stood still. It was a holy moment. Lynn fit me just like Annie: both were five feet four inches and weighed the same. Annie also had a country-and-western body. And by the luscious grace of God, it was being held against me. The first embrace in over two years. This was an utterly genuine "Oh my Lord and my God!" moment. It was not sexual, but gloriously sensual. Lynn was the shoulder and arms, hands and bosom, waist and legs for Jesus that night. My shredded body and soul seemed to be totally healed for the moment. Pain and anxiety rushed from my head and flushed from my body, leaving me feeling light and free. A momentary transcendence and the beginning of a beautiful and wholesome friendship that remains to this day.

⌐ • ⌐

School continued to provide perfect cover: it distracted my mind a bit and served to reduce the distress I felt for not holding down a job. I was matriculating at a full-time pace, even though the majority of my time and energy went toward the Lord and his ways. Once I got comfortable with the classroom dynamics and the academic game, I maintained a 4.0 GPA.

Lynn was no small part of this successful dynamic, and in spite of the Lord's ways being easy and his burden light, my developing relationship with her had its own challenges. Lynn and I were natural playmates, and since we had no parents who were available to schedule a playdate, we decided to do so on our own. She, it turned out, owned a hair salon and was a full-time hair stylist with five women subcontracting with her. For my part, I was a middle-aged man in need of a good haircut. The fact that Lynn was also a barber facilitated our plan.

Lynn's fiancé, Steve, had scheduled an extensive hunting trip to the wilds of Canada. This left Lynn with some free time, and she suggested that we meet on a Sunday afternoon and she would give me a first-rate haircut. As I waited in the parking lot of the strip mall in Gurnee, Illinois, Lynn rolled up in her little blue Nissan pickup. She hopped out with keys in hand and beckoned me toward the locked door of her salon. I was soon in the styling chair, and we were discussing good hair options. I gave her my thoughts, and she proceeded to produce a result that was better than I had hoped for.

The day was still young, so Lynn suggested that she show me around the area. We stopped by her girlhood home, where her brother and his family now lived, along with her grandpa. We then checked out her current house, which was undergoing a big remodeling effort (having been an Al Capone roadhouse in the past). From the Chain of Lakes region, where Lynn chauffeured us past a rental that she had owned, we headed east toward a harbor on Lake Michigan. We walked out and sat on a long breakwater, with the water some twenty feet below us. There she began to tell me her story—and a compelling story it was. She said that she could look back and see God at work in the life of a young girl who grew up under mostly secular influences. Trusting in Jesus in her late teens, she went on to experience some of the horror stories that have generally disillusioned those who are victims of Christian youth leadership. But Lynn had continued with the Lord, even though her relationship with the church had suffered some.

Heading north after gassing up her pickup, we ended up dining on pizza al fresco in Kenosha, Wisconsin. The sun was starting to fade as we finished off our beers and headed back to Gurnee. It had been an unforgettable day.

But I had one lingering issue, which was the apostle Paul's admonition in 1 Corinthians 5:11: "But now I have written to you not to keep company with anyone named a brother [or sister], who is sexually immoral, or covetous, or an idolater, or a reviler, or a drunkard, or an extortioner—not even to eat with such a person." I had been aware of it for some time, since Lynn was an up-front person and hadn't hidden it from me in our class and after-class conversations. I knew that she and Steve were shacking up, or, as some in the Christian community would say, "living in sin." I wasn't personally offended by this. It's easy to understand the fifty-year impetus of America's sexual revolution when, for years before, the testimony of many Christians was a "thou-shalt-not" attitude toward anything fun in life—let alone sinful.

As a young, impetuous teenager, I was thankful for the conversation I had had with my father. He explained that society would come apart at the seams if sexual activity deviated from the protection of the ideal of a lifetime marriage contract. So, even though shacking up on an individual basis might seem innocuous, it was easy to understand and also to observe the detriment to society. God wanted us to love our neighbor, not have sex with him or her, and in so doing protect the whole family structure.

My concern was a little different. I was aware of biblical prohibitions against socializing with fornicators, of sharing in the fellowship of a meal with them. Though the biblical word for "fornication" suggests a militant attitude toward generally more destructive behaviors, I knew that God still wanted the marriage bed honored. By the same token, in the reckoning of many cultures, Lynn was monogamous and married—the marriage just hadn't been celebrated yet. The commitment was there, just not the ceremony. In

America we have acknowledged this with the concept of common-law marriage.

My life was in such a fix that I couldn't afford to have God aggravated with me for negligent behavior. At the same time, Lynn ranked right up there in the pantheon of people who ever meant much to me. Presently, she was also the best therapy for my soul aside from Jesus, Cal (my counselor), and my sisters. What to think? Well, I wasn't sure, but I went to the Lord and took full responsibility. I told him I spent forty years rejecting people based on someone else's biblical interpretations, and I was going to spend the next forty trying to love people. I also cited Jesus's inclination to spend time with sinners and give churchy types short shrift. I was going to show up at dinner with Lynn, with Jesus at my side, and hope that the two of us would have more influence in her life going forward.

CHAPTER 21
TRAINED BY PAIN

*Who [Jesus], in the days of his flesh, when he offered up
prayers and supplications, with vehement cries and tears to
him who was able to save him from death, and was heard
because of his godly fear, though he was a son, yet he learned
obedience by the things which he suffered.*
—Hebrews 5:7–8

*My son, do not despise the chastening of the Lord, nor detest
his correction; For whom the Lord loves he corrects, just as a
father the son in whom he delights.*
—Proverbs 3:11–12

*I in them and you in me; that they may be made perfect in one,
and that the world may know that you have sent me and have
loved them as you have loved me. Father, I desire that they
also whom you gave me may be with me where I am, that they
may behold my glory which you have given me; for you loved
me before the foundation of the world.*
—John 17:23–24

*For both he who sanctifies and those who are being sanctified
are all of one, for which reason he is not ashamed to call them
brethren, saying, "I will declare your name to my brethren."
And again: "Here am I and the children whom God has*

given me."
—Hebrews 2:11, 13

G od knows that the things we learn and experience in childhood are hard to shake. He took me off the grid with the pain and grief of my divorce, but in his love for me, he desired that I lay all of my baggage down. He knew just how to heal my wounds. He opened his Word and astounded me with what I heard next. The writer of Hebrews (5:7) speaks of Jesus in his whole, perfect humanity, offering up prayers to Abba with tears, of his prayers heard, but learning obedience through the *things that he suffered*. Absolutely mind-blowing! A perfect man praying, a perfect man crying, a perfect man learning, and a perfect man getting whacked.

I took a deep breath. I had thought God-inflicted pain was punitive, a tit-for-tat mechanism for getting even. Where tacit fellowship had existed in my childhood, it was totally upheaved in punishment, and never explicitly restored. I would walk on eggshells, hoping not to upset the status quo again anytime soon. Instead, I am reading now of a Father inflicting suffering on a totally sinless son in order to strengthen his character to enable him to bear our sins without fear of failure or any second thoughts. The Father meant him no harm: this was not punitive; it was love strengthening his son for the joy that was set before him. And to think the Son of God had to learn all this through suffering.

God was breaking in and breaking down the notion that all pain is punitive. He was just getting started. In Hebrews 12, pain was once again not an issue of retribution; rather, it was correction and instruction, a sign of a father's love, administered for my benefit. I had heard God referred to as Father as far back as my memory stretched. Okay, so what? Fathers sat all night in their easy chair and read the newspaper, caressing and massaging every line and every word. Fathers were not to be bothered with trivial things like children. They worked hard and were entitled to be left alone. If you screwed up your courage to implore him by saying "Dad," hoping that, if he did lift up his countenance, he would grant you peace, it was more likely that he never heard you. Happy Father's Day!

The God of the universe claims me as his son and speaks of his delight in me. He delights in me! Wait! Stop! No, look it up: Proverbs 3:12 intimates nothing less. Any pain only reinforces God's delight in me. Not performance-based and beyond well-pleased, he takes great pleasure in me. I bring him joy, satisfaction, gratification because I am his son. In his infinite love, he can love me as if I were the only person that exists.

The depth of God's genius is mesmerizing. He tells us that we will not like pain. He tells us that Jesus didn't like the thought of pain either. Yet in his sovereign love, he either directly administers or allows pain, so much so that it even happens to the perfect human, Jesus. Perfection can't deserve punishment. Jesus was not being punished. There is no condemnation for those in Christ Jesus. Our pain is not punitive. The writer of Hebrews says pain sets us apart to God, that is, in holiness. Jesus and his siblings are being trained to experience the beauty of God, even his righteousness.

Jesus was trained by pain to such an extent that when they spit, mocked, beat, and punished him, he was able to say, "Father, forgive them, for they know not what they do." And when he bore in his own body every sin ever committed, and he experienced the guilt, shame, and punishment of sins he had no affinity with, he took it and ushered in the love of God to a dead and dying world. Jesus, in his deity, was called from the perfect company of the Trinity in eternity, where pain didn't exist, into time and a world of sin that created pain. God then flipped pain into a mechanism for the soul expansion of Jesus and us. One has to wonder, did Jesus have a more magnificent view of God after the cross? Were his senses heightened for all eternity to see God in every crack and crevice of his human spirit and soul by the sheer madness on the cross?

Pain most often diminishes the recipient. God's intent is to use pain to expand the human soul. His desire is to enlarge the soul in order to possess his love for the world and, by congruence, absorb his infinite love for us. Where have I been all my life? I sat and soaked this in until I fell asleep, content in the arms of my Father.

⌣ • ⌣

Soon, I again sat with the book of Hebrews open in front of me. Still astounded by a sinless person learning obedience, my attention was drawn to Hebrews 12:12. There the writer commands his readers to "strengthen the hands that hang down." Usually this made me think of the cult interpretation: that the readers of the book were about to die the "sin unto death," and that they needed to repent and get back on track. Instead, this time I was transported back to the image of me as a nine-year-old boy in a hospital bed with a broken arm set in a cast, hanging from a pole in traction alongside me. It was an unsettling and painful experience for a small boy, to say the least, until somewhere into my second day in the hospital, my biggest brother (eighteen years older than me) walked in with a chocolate milkshake hidden under his right arm. He handed me the contraband, and I began to pull it through a big straw.

Content in the company of the best big brother a kid could ever hope for, I relaxed. But my brother's work was calling, and soon he had to leave. Shortly after that, the army called him back to active duty, and he was gone — never to return for more than a day or two at a time. I saw little of him for the next thirteen years. Then, just six weeks after my own active duty in the army ended, I moved in with my brother, sister-in-law, and three nieces. Finally reunited with my big brother after all those years, I was basking in his company. We worked side by side each day, enjoying our coffee on the way to work each morning and reading the newspaper each night, our workday ending long after everyone had gone to bed. But eight weeks after our new relationship had enlivened my life, we were all shocked by his sudden death. In little more than an instant, the Lord had called him home. As I sat in my study some twenty-five years later, I could finally admit that a chunk of me had died that day. As the tears rolled down my cheeks, I questioned the necessity of such a vivid reminder.

But God has his ways. Quickly and quietly he turned me around in the book to Hebrews 2:11. It was here that the Holy Spirit gave me Jesus as my Big Brother! The text says that both "he who sanctifies (Jesus) and those who are being sanctified (us) are all of one [Father], for which reason he [Jesus] is not ashamed to call them brethren." What an incredible reality! Jesus looked at his Daddy, looked at me, and said, "We're brothers, Garry, we're brothers!" It started me thinking about what it meant to have a big brother. I immediately had someone I could count on: undying loyalty from my brother who died for me. Someone who liked me, loved me, looked out for me! And someone I could talk to.

Holy Spirit caused me to recall John 17, where Jesus asks the Father to share the same love he had for Jesus, so Jesus could share it with me. Elsewhere he declares: "If you have seen me, you have seen the Father." Wow, Jesus is who God wants to be seen as—my big brother, the face of God. The churches I had sat in for most of my life denied me the privilege of talking to Jesus. You prayed to the Father, in the name of the Son, through the Holy Spirit. Well, hallelujah, world without end, amen! It was nothing more than a theological exercise, reducing God to a concept and leaving a person talking to the sky, the ceiling, or himself. Now I had a real live person who was claiming me as brother, introducing me to our Daddy, and wanting to be with me. In fact, he went to prepare a place for me, a place where he is and I can be also. I was going to have a big brother for time and eternity.

After I had suffered the rejection, abandonment, and self-loathing that came with the betrayal of divorce, my big brother knew exactly what I needed. He gave me family, and he gave me the biggest promise he could in Hebrews 13:5: "I will never, ever, ever leave or forsake you." Together now and forever—thank you, Jesus.

CHAPTER 22
WE ARE FAMILY

"Do I have any pleasure at all that the wicked should die?"
says the Lord God, "and not that he shall turn from his ways
and live?"
—Ezekiel 18:23

The Lord used school to create another soul-challenging opportunity, which I didn't relish any more than trying to figure out how to conduct my affairs with Lynn. Consistent with my Van Til bloodlines, I had spent my life around the Bible, and my adulthood heavily invested in theology, doctrine, and biblical Greek and Hebrew. With that background, I figured the quickest way to the goal line of my undergraduate degree was to combine a minor in biblical studies with my communications major. As my communications studies continued, I embarked in a basic course on the Old Testament.

While I was trying to accelerate these endeavors, up jumped the ghosts of my childhood. Knowing that Old Testament studies is where the Calvinist professors are usually embedded, I planned to quietly take the course. This hope quickly faded. I soon discovered that my professor was a man in transition. He had recently taught at my alma mater, Illiana Christian High School, and he was chomping at the bit to do doctoral studies at Westminster Seminary in Philadelphia, where my great-uncle Cornelius Van Til was a legend. My prof literally worshiped at my great-uncle's seat—his chair, that is. One of his students at the high school was my somewhat distant cousin. I didn't know who she was, but if she was related to the great Cornelius and her last name was Van Til, she was related to me. Apparently, Van Til had visited her parents, as he had occasionally visited mine, and in so doing he had sat in one of their chairs. When he learned of this, my professor requested the opportunity to worship at such a shrine. She graciously granted his request and invited him to her house, where he reposed in said chair and contemplated his good fortune.

My classroom interaction with our professor somehow required that I reconsider my childhood beliefs. At first I thought that perhaps my weakened emotional state—or the weight of almost 500 years of Reformed history—forced the review. Later I would realize it was not a crisis of faith, but a crisis of person, that precipitated my quandary. Even as Annie's rejection had initiated the great question of who I ultimately was, so now it was spilling over into a whole other arena.

I had no desire to engage in any debate with a Calvinist or with Calvinism in general. I thought that I had put all those questions to rest more than thirty years earlier, when R. B. Thieme's ministry had given me confident answers to all the questions of my youth. Furthermore, if you plan on facing off with a Calvinist, my advice is, "Don't bring a knife to a gunfight." My experience growing up suggested that my forebears' theology was planted in neatly gardened rows in the fertile soil of their minds. I would venture to say Calvinist theologians are the most studied and developed in their discipline. Not only did I have a world-renowned great-uncle, but my mother had at least two brothers of high rank among the theology professors

that graced the classrooms of two of the more prominent Christian Reformed colleges and seminaries. Semi-
recreational reading in our house would not only include
Cornelius Van Til's *Defense of the Faith*, but also my Uncle
Hank's (Henry Van Til) *The Calvinistic Concept of Culture*.
Animated conversations at family get-togethers at our house
could produce such intriguing thoughts that one uncle or
another might be seen tapping his cigar ashes into the cuff
of his pants, lest he need to withdraw from the conversation
in search of an ashtray. Some of my Van Til uncles (the ones
who used tobacco), came with their smoking pipes in hand
and never had to leave the discussion.

At a personal level, this was family. In theory, God may
have been number one in our orbit, but, practically speaking,
this played out as love for family. I grew up with great
admiration for my siblings and respect for my parents and
their roots. God may have been mean and boring, but the
Leeps and Van Tils were pretty cool. I liked most of them
and was proud to be one. Before it had been minted and
placed on bumper stickers, I had unconsciously subscribed
to the statement "If you ain't Dutch, you ain't much."

To this day, I get a smile on my face when I think of
Uncle Kees: not only did he comport himself as a kind and
gracious man when he came to visit my bedridden mother;
you can also see these qualities in any photograph you might
find when you Google his name. When I had taken summer
sessions of Greek years earlier at Grace Seminary, I had
kicked up a covey of young Calvinists. As we took a break
during our three-hour morning class, we would retreat from
the seminary to a building with a bank of vending machines.
As I inserted my coins to draw a cup of coffee, I could hear
a tableful of young men engaged in what sounded like a
debate as to whether my great-uncle smoked a cigar and

whether he would smoke it in his offices at Westminster Seminary. (Smoking, drinking, dancing, going to movies, and playing cards were strictly forbidden at Grace College and Seminary.) I turned toward their table and inquired whether that was indeed what they were talking about. They nodded in the affirmative, while wondering who I might be and what possible audacity I might possess to invade their conversation. I proceeded to inform them that Van Til never smoked his cigars while visiting my mother (where he had been within the last few weeks), but I could think of no reason that would prohibit him from smoking in the privacy of his own office. They cocked their heads, like quizzical dogs looking at their master, and asked me how I knew Van Til. "He's my great-uncle," I replied. They arose from their chairs to shake my hand, likely wondering if something good would rub off. One of them concluded, "So you're a Calvinist, right?" (they were a small minority on campus at the time). I looked at him and said, "No, I think I'm what you refer to as a Thiemite," which was, in their estimation, closely related to a termite. They turned and headed back to our classroom, never to utter another word to me.

My rather stern grandpa sometimes showed a softer side, of which I was occasionally privileged to be the recipient. On visiting my mother, he asked if I (still a young boy) would like to stay overnight at his house. Though I was on alert, my mother assured me it would be just fine. The next morning Grandma made us breakfast, after which I had to wait patiently while Grandpa read his Bible and then some articles from the church's magazine. Finally, we launched outdoors to do something active. We proceeded to build a new and spacious doghouse for his beautiful collie. Grandpa settled into the project and manifested himself to be quite engaging, even with a nine- or ten-year-old. Later

Grandma called us in for lunch, but before we retired to the house, Grandpa had to show me how he had rigged the passenger-side door on his car so that it always remained locked and only could be opened from the inside. That was in the days before seat belts, and he did not want Grandma rolling out of the car by accident; plus, he was preventing the chance (an unlikely chance back then) of someone ripping open the door in a threatening way.

Starting out in life, I had been a mama's boy, trying to please her in all that I did. It was what I thought was expected of me, and it didn't cause me much distress. But soon, though my dad was very quiet, I wanted to be around him. My dad, Curly Leep, was built like a beer barrel as a result of tossing around eight-gallon cans of milk (approximately ninety pounds) for many years; but his mind was even more robust. Though his formal education only went through the fifth grade on the open expanses of the Saskatchewan prairie, he was a practical intellectual. His life had started in Chicago, but his father, Grandpa Leep, had decided to heed an opportunity to homestead on the Canadian prairie. His hope was to raise his family in a more wholesome environment than what early twentieth-century Chicago offered, and in Canada he could acquire a homestead after several years of toil. At first things went well in the heavily Dutch-settled community near Swift Current, Saskatchewan; but within a few years the homesteaders were planting more wheat seed than they were harvesting. Eventually, after a number of years of drought, the dream disintegrated, and my dad returned to the Chicago area (northwest Indiana) along with his parents and eight of nine surviving siblings.

The Leeps were a spirited people: lively, colorful, and salt of the earth. Whereas some of the Van Tils distinguished themselves academically, the Leeps had a more commercial bent. Necessity, often the force that spurs one toward great success, was at work in my Uncle Bud's life. After investing his labors in a dairy-farm operation, he could not find any dairy willing to allow him to make a profit on his milk production. He soon decided to launch into the sale of his milk at the retail level, and Pleasant View Dairy went from being a farm to a commercial dairy. Back in the late 1920s and early 1930s, Pleasant View was one of over a hundred dairy operations in Lake County, Indiana. By the time the 1970s rolled around, Pleasant View was the last operation standing, and it remains to this day a boutique dairy offering the freshest milk available beyond the farm. Though we mostly drank his milk out of bottles (the best vehicle for the flavor of milk), it was fun to read the side of a paper milk carton, where on one side was an ode to Pleasant View's world-champion Brown Swiss cow, Lady Gypsy Girl, and on another side a gentle message enjoining the milk drinker to attend the church of his choice that weekend.

It was, in fact, Uncle Bud's personal stature that created within me a desire to be a millionaire. He was never a slave to riches; rather, because of his character and modeling, I thought that wealth required great personal integrity. I soon discovered, in life beyond my uncle, that the two are not synonymous.

Aunt Cy—now she was a character who gave me hope. When it was past my bedtime, perhaps during a birthday celebration for my dad, when his siblings and their spouses would congregate in our kitchen around my mother's fine desserts, I would hear—amongst the rumblings of the conversation—my aunt suddenly break out in a loud cackle. Somehow this, in a world where most of my elders seemed as serious as a heart attack, gave me hope that some happiness could yet be found in my future life as an adult. And my Uncle Jim, having been divorced some years before, would come to visit on a warm summer day and then would ask my mother if it would be okay to take us kids (Patricia and me) to Wrigley Field for a Cubs game. Yes! Definitely okay.

But these relatives were not short in their own adoration of God. As far back as the 1950s, Aunt Eve launched an evening of sing-along Christmas carols on the first Sunday in December. What had started out in her living room morphed into a grand gathering in the church basement that often attracted more than eighty offspring of my Grandpa Leep—and continued for over fifty years. These were my people, and I liked them; but for more than forty years I could find no solace in their view of God.

It reminded me of one of the great joys of my boyhood, growing up in a two-and-a-half-acre sandbox, the beautiful sand, the likely remnant of a postglacial Lake Michigan shoreline that now has receded some five miles to its present configuration. On a warm summer day, we would romp and run all morning and afternoon, but when it was time for lunch or supper, before we set foot in our *hokkie* (the Dutch word for a small mudroom), our mother would admonish us to empty the sand from our shoes. Sometimes we had already been compelled to remove them in order to dump the accumulation of sand. The fine sand would build up under our heels and arches, making walking painful, especially once we reached something harder than the soft sand. And now, as an adult, I found more than sand in my shoes; indeed, there were sharp little stones, those scruples that I had inadvertently kicked up, likely with the Lord's providential aid.

So off I went on a theological journey, despite the fact that God had illuminated himself in my life as a kind and considerate person toward all humanity. As I turned my mind toward the word of God, the Word of God— the Logos, yes, Jesus—turned his heart toward me. I reviewed many Reformed positions and their proof-texts. I scoured the Bible, reviewing such subjects as election, predestination, and the logical sequence of God's thinking. I considered prevenient grace and even the views of Uncle Kees from the lofty mount of presuppositional apologetics and theology. For a while, it was more stimulating than a good bridge game, but eventually so unnecessary.

As I was doing my homework, Holy Spirit of Jesus was asking me when he ever acted like this. "When was I so impoverished of soul that I would only die for some when I had the assets to die for all? Why would I give humanity a conscience with a sense of fairness and justice and then so utterly violate it by arbitrarily consigning the bulk of humanity to eternal damnation? Does my behavior suggest that your mother had a greater love for her children than I do for my creation? Do I take pleasure in the death of the wicked? Do I not long for the wicked to turn from their ways? Aren't all the choices given in the Bible testimony to volition, or am I playing everybody? Can't I do all the work of salvation and have it rejected, even as Christians can grieve and quench Holy Spirit by personal choice? How could you ever begin to understand the injunction to be "imitators of Christ" under anything else than all-embracing love? Is not my glory in my graciousness?"

I smiled as I basked in the beauty of God's love. My earthly father had championed the small man, the underdog. He would fight for him philosophically in the arena of economics, trying to persuade anyone who would listen that the God of Scripture was for the little guy. I had discovered that my emotional and mental makeup resembled his in many ways. And even here, my take on the underdog was similar to his. After all, what greater underdog could there be than the one Jesus hadn't died for!

It was an intense time with Jesus, another good day with the ultimate big brother. My thinking was once again grounded in the Word. And before I headed off to class, he whispered another bit of advice: "Don't debate with them, Garry, for as you do, it will lock the door of their mind and throw away the key to their heart."

CHAPTER 23
YOU BELONG TO ME

*For you, O God, have tested us; you have refined us as silver is
refined. You brought us into the net; you laid affliction on our
backs. You have caused men to ride over our heads; we went
through fire and through water; but you brought us out to rich
fulfillment.*
—Psalm 66:10–12

*You have tested my heart; you have visited me in the night; you
have tried me and have found nothing; I have purposed that
my mouth shall not transgress.*
—Psalm 17:3

*Now Gideon perceived that He was the Angel of the Lord, so
Gideon said, "Alas, O Lord God! For I have seen the Angel of
the Lord face to face." Then the Lord said to him, "Peace be
with you: do not fear, you shall not die."*
—Judges 6:22–23

P ain has a way of confusing one's thinking. Early in my
grief, the confusion was moment by moment, minute
by minute, hour by hour, a relentless assault on my soul.
Any certainty I had built my life around became unsure.
Like a battlefield scene in the din of war, disorientation
came easy, stability was fleeting. Now life began inching
toward normality. Suicidal impulses were lessening. I could

go for a two-mile walk and not return home in full panic mode. There was time to shave and shower before engaging with Holy Spirit and the Word. My pain-relieving tears each morning had diminished from two or three hours to under one. My classmate Lynn's weekly hugs were as comforting as ever, leaving me less unsettled after the rigor of four hours with people. My life was slowly becoming less about what I had lost, but—in a surreal way—more an experience of being lost. The trauma required more of me; I had to become more. But how? I was totally stuck.

When sleep was interrupted by pain, I had developed the habit of getting on my knees at the foot-end of my bed. Affording my knees some padding on the carpeting, this position provided a way to concentrate as I poured out my heart to God, asking for immediate relief from my sorrows. I had been fighting for my physical life all this time, trying to stave off the impulses of a tortured soul. Now, in the middle of the night, when I usually found some fleeting rest, here comes God—wanting my soul. I am the skeptical type when it comes to these kinds of experiences. I would probably deny that it happened, except that the results were so overwhelming as to be personally undeniable. What happened next is still a mystery to me: the best word I have been able to find to describe it is "phantasmagorical." It wasn't physical, because I was still at the end of the bed; it wasn't a dream, because I was wide awake.

It seemed in my mind that I was suddenly clinging to the inside of a deep well, from whose depths there could be no rescue. As I clung, hoping for rescue, a message from God was telling me to let go. I was overwhelmed with despair. He wasn't there to rescue me; he had only sent a message to let go. I hung on for dear life! No one was there to rescue me, not even Jesus, and I realized that I couldn't hold out much longer. Nearing my end, I let go!

I don't remember falling, but I was suddenly in a welcoming, sunny, bright, comfortable, modern place. It was wondrous! I cannot say whether it was indoors or outdoors, but, like an open-air arena, it was spacious. There was a vibe of active tranquility. I don't remember any people present, but I certainly didn't feel alone. I was surrounded by love. A moment later, I was again at the end of my bed. I remained kneeling—staggered and in a daze—but mostly I felt drained by the fear I had felt about the prospect of falling to a lonely, inescapable death in the bottom of a dark, cold, and watery grave. The joy would come in the morning.

Whatever happened during the night remained with me the next morning. It was unforgettable. And the result had been so beautiful that the experience became less frightening to think about. I even smiled for a moment as I remembered the derisive comments people in the cult made about people who uttered clichés like "Let go and let God." I didn't know what other folks had been referring to, but this was the ultimate "let go," with no assurances from God. When I decided to let go, I had nothing more left; it was the all of me. There was no more begging, bargaining, or borrowing: I was giving up my life without any sense of a rescue. I was "letting go" *in obedience* to God. The transaction turned out to be absolutely transformational. Looking back, it was giving up self-Garry and gaining God. I had, as they say, "surrendered," and, unbeknownst to me, I was taken hostage by Love—for God *is* Love.

I had had many illuminations by Holy Spirit over the years, paradigm shifts that sent me back to the Bible, knowing that I would have to reevaluate everything in light of what had been revealed to me. This was incomparably different. I had been in the presence of God. Self-Garry had been consumed when God revealed himself as Love. I was about to embark on an explosive tour of the Bible, God revealing himself as a lover beyond description.

For the moment, still deep in pain, I was beginning to feel that it was all worth it. I had been given something more than I had ever expected. He was now my God, because I was now his! I knew I could never find my way out of my pain, but I relaxed a little. God was right there with me, and God is Love.

⌐ • ⌐

As I sat with the Lord and his Word, my eyes rested on Psalm 139:14. David speaks of being "fearfully and wonderfully made." It reminded me of when I was young and our choices of translations were slim and the King James Version. Was the Bible full of contradictions? At first glance, "fearful" and "wonderful" are worlds apart. Why did the Bible traffic in fear so much, even in such a glad moment? And why did the behavior of my elders suggest that asking a question when I was baffled could be irreverent and might get me squashed?

Although my Christian environment had become more relaxed and loving, none of the pastors were inclined to put the fear of God in proper context. Apparently, at some level, they also grew up with a God to fear. The "fear of God" seemed to be the third rail of biblical teaching: you touch it, you die. Like a stand of tall hardwoods, the "fear of God" was a mighty obstacle in my life. How do you love and fear the same person? The Lord wanted me to take an ax to these perplexities at their roots.

The first swing of the ax took me to I John 4:18. Here the apostle speaks some reassuring words: "There is no fear in love; but perfect [mature] love casts out fear," because fear involves torment (punishment). Aha, I was correct: love and fear are mutually exclusive. You cannot fully love where fear resides. The whole impetus of the "Christian construct" of my youth was false. As I leaned back in my chair, trying to absorb some of the fullness of this reality, my mind drifted back to an experience from years before.

After a day filled with sales calls, I was headed home in my jet-black, short-bed Ford F-150. Sunshine still filled the sky as I sped along U.S. Highway 31. I began to slow as the traffic lights that controlled the flow in and around Grissom Air Force base began to appear. Always interested in the activity beyond the security fence, I strained my neck and eyes to see if there were any aircraft staging for takeoff. Just as I began to brake for the light, I felt a tremor. My first thought was that something was wrong with my brakes. The ensuing noise and violence erased such a notion. The road seemed to upheave and the truck shook, vibrated, and rattled like an old rusted-out jalopy. It felt and sounded like hail was coming down on the roof.

My mind was momentarily numbed as my truck rolled out of the epicenter of the concussion. Recovering my senses, I looked off to my right. There was a B-52 at less than a hundred feet, exhaust billowing from its eight engines, pulling a full-throttle aborted landing, a possible touch-and-go exercise. If I had seen the massive bomber coming in over my truck, I likely would have peed my pants. I was totally awestruck. Had I been afoot, I surely would have dropped to my knees. The power, though never intended for my harm, was overwhelming.

We have a God who is so totally magnificent in character, in fullness of person, that to be finite in the presence of that glorious infinity, to be creature in the presence of the Creator, is to experience Godly fear. Not fear of torment, punishment, rejection, or hell, but an openness to the experience of mind-altering realities that reverberate throughout eternity. Indeed, our God is so awesome that every knee will buckle, every tongue will confess that Jesus Christ is Lord. The magnitude of his person leaves no other options: to stand in his presence is to bow, if not in adoration, surely in capitulation to our finite limitations. Was this fearful? Not in the way I had been taught fear. In the words of our culture's youth, it was "totally awesome." Thanks, kids. Indeed, we have a totally awesome God!

The Lord had another point to make. He is not the God of fear, but the "fear not" God. When Jesus appeared to mankind—be it a theophany, Christophany, or some other manifestation—were not the first words he uttered to the startled and stunned witnesses, "Fear not"? After all those years with some form of "godly fear" hanging over my head, it was a great comfort to realize that our gracious God, when buckling the knees of human beings with his unexpected appearances, uttered such soothing words as "do not fear," "do not be afraid," and "fear not." As I began to peruse these citations from Genesis to Revelation, the goodness of God overwhelmed me with gratitude. He had no intent to scare the bejabbers out of these people. Instead, he is a God worthy of our awe who absorbs our fears in the bosom of his love.

It became evident to me that all this "fear" stuff was a matter of definitions that had grown obsolete. Even though the word "fear" as a literal translation from the original text might have been accurate in the context of King James and his linguistic team, a teenager's use of the words "totally awesome" might be a more accurate translation in the culture of the twenty-first century (though when a teenager at a grocery checkout calls your sunglasses "awesome," the word has lost some of its depth of meaning). It was time to put this fear stuff to rest and luxuriate in the worship of a totally awesome God.

CHAPTER 24
SAVE THE FIRST DANCE FOR ME

He has delivered us from the power of darkness and conveyed us into the kingdom of the Son of his love.
—Colossians 1:13.

For by him all things are created.
—Colossians 1:16.

As I have previously mentioned, the God of my youth was foreboding. Whether it was God in a movie talking to Moses, or God on a Bill Cosby record talking to Noah, or God stalking Adam in the garden of Eden asking, "Where are you?"—he was no-nonsense and certainly not to be trifled with. I knew at a young age that we were created to glorify God, whatever that meant. It was hard to understand. God did whatever he pleased, creating a person and then sovereignly choosing to make him a sinner by birth, but not willing to provide salvation for him in Christ. Created + damned= glory to God! This was not an equation that was easy to live by.

Escaping this math at twenty, I heard the new math as explained by the cult: that we were created to settle the angelic conflict. In Satan's rebellion, he supposedly indicted God's fairness for banishing him to hell. This led

God to create a lower creature, yet with volition, so that Satan could observe man choose freely for God. This would settle the argument on terms Satan could readily understand. We were simply pawns in God's chess match with Satan. Also, explicit in the discussion was the fact that God did not need us; he is infinite. Infinity has no needs outside itself: the three persons of the Godhead had infinite community, and God was not lonely; he was plenty happy without us. By all appearances, we were no more important than another child in a house already overrun with them. Not wanted, dead or alive.

As I pondered these things, the Lord gave me a fresh and beautiful panorama to behold. He interjected: "Let's back this up a bit before the churchmen gave you that forty years of total depravity and 'no damn good' stuff. Let's go back to the dawn of creation. Has it not been said, 'All things were created by him and for him (Jesus)'? Can you imagine my perfect Son creating something that is less than perfect? What can a person of infinite love create that doesn't have infinite value? And what could be created *for him* of less than infinite value? Do you somehow think your sins destroyed your infinite value to Infinite Love? To be loved is to be valued, and to be valued by Infinite Love is to have infinite value.

"Garry, do you realize that you are a gift of infinite value to my Son? We stood in eternity—with everything! What does a God who has everything give to a God who has everything? A dance! We conspired between us to speak *you* out of our eternal love into time, forever altering reality. We danced, we cavorted, we played; you were born. Born from our lovemaking into time. Born in the image of a playful God!

"The Son and the Spirit and I—we reveled in the joy of creation. It was pure pleasure to design and create. Satan and his cohorts had made a mess of things, and we began to clean things up. We brought forth light, and what a game changer that was! Then we rolled out one new thing after another, and it was all the best. But then, then we had some real fun. We made Adam, and then Eve—what a masterpiece my Son built! Incredible, astonishing, a totally awesome soul mate for Adam. We couldn't wait to see his reaction.

"And now, Garry, listen closely, for here is the rest of the story: In the garden I was God and man was man. I called him son, and we had our thing where I visited in the cool of the evening. Father/son and daughter, you know. And then it happened: Adam was standing on the threshold of eternal life, but he brought down a kingdom. The universe shuddered in pain. The Son put forth more energy to sustain it. The oceans writhed and roiled. Where formally the animals munched on herbs and vegetation together, now there lay the blood-soaked carcass of a rabbit, torn apart by the fox, now slinking away.

"The brilliance of all the colors of Paradise were dimmed. Stars began their slow demise. Looking forward, I saw a multitude reject the joy of true worship for the torture of an eternity without fellowship with their Creator. I saw the dismay, the disheartened throngs, longing for solace, and I saw them deny my existence because of the sheer violence and poverty of their world and lives. I saw them cower, I saw them cringe; my Adam was gone. The dance, Garry, the dance was over. We had talked about it for all eternity. We three are totally fulfilled within one another, totally synchronized in our sovereignty. Totally whole!

"And then we chose to bring into existence by him, through him, and for him, a creation that would dance with the eternal. In the gifting of God to each other, man was the center, the plaything, the joy of our universe, the extravagance of our love. Now, now he was gone. Lost, they began to hide. I came looking for them. Most bible commentators make it sound foreboding, like I was mad. No way! I was distressed and I was grieving. My son and daughter had fallen prey to Satan. I cried out, 'Adam, where are you? My son, my son!' It was an OMA (Oh My Adam) moment. I would have torn my hair out if I had any; I would have ripped my clothes off in grief if I wore any.

"But you know how all things work together for good for those who love God? Well, here comes the good part. Garry, in our dance, in our communion, in our lovemaking, we decided to forever alter our reality. We had determined to become man, God-man, yes to save humanity, but more importantly to include you in our dance. The humanity of God, in its perfection, has all the normal human needs, including wholesome emotional needs. And my Son chose to become Jesus (human), and he will forever desire you: the joy that was set before him, the reason he endured the cross, suffered the shame of your sins, and now waits with me until the wedding feast of the Lamb, when the dance will be on! Welcome to our dance!"

My Lord and My God!

CHAPTER 25
A GUT-WRENCHED GOD

And Jesus, when he came out, saw a great multitude and was moved with compassion for them, because they were like sheep not having a shepherd. So he began to teach them many things.
—Mark 6:34

And when Jesus went out he saw a great multitude; he was moved with compassion for them and healed their sick.
—Matthew 14:14

Surely, he has borne our griefs and carried our sorrows. And he shall divide the spoil with the strong, because he poured out his soul unto death.
—Isaiah 53:4, 12

A thletes refer to it as choking. When they are under pressure, you can sometimes see them pulling at their shirt tops. Semi-drivers, when they have overdriven a situation, refer to it in rather colorful terms. Personally, I had felt like someone had wrenched my stomach right up against my throat, leaving little room to breathe and virtually no room to eat. As I had progressed away from this despair to deep depression, my chokehold had begun to abate. Other than forty pounds of depression-influenced weight gain, it had been life-saving. Now a little farther from the inferno, the Lord brought new hope to my soul.

Perusing the Psalms, my go-to book for pain-relief, my eyes rested on the words of David in Psalm 145. In the eighth verse he begins: "The Lord is gracious and full of compassion, slow to anger and great in mercy." Verse nine: "The Lord is good to all, and his tender mercies are over all his works." I sat, stunned once again by what a good-natured God I had. My mind drifted back to a story my mother told when I was just a "wee boy," as the Irish might say. And it was an Irish tale of sorts that she told.

Apparently, the song "Danny Boy" had gained (or regained) popularity in America during the 1950s. The Dutch Reformed had a song in their Psalter Hymnal that was sung to the same Londonderry Aire tune. It is a beautiful hymn, its lyrics influenced by Psalm 103, which portrays God as being good and full of kind compassion. The majesty of God as a tender and kind Father is emotionally overwhelming; coupled with the beautiful "Danny Boy" tune, it is a song hard to parallel in its beauty. But it was ripped from the pages of the church's next edition of the hymnbook by the church authorities, never more to be seen, because "Danny Boy," as wonderful a song as it was in its own right, was a secular song. The church, likely feeling some compromise with the world, must have felt a godly obligation to excise "Good is the Lord and Full of Kind Compassion." I'm sure Satan laughed with glee. As I read the words in the old red hymnal, perplexity once again filled my head. In my youth, the God of our songbook was not the God of our church pew. How could we have such reassuring words of a wonderful and beautiful God in our songs, but nothing comparable in our lives? As I wrestled a bit, my Abba wanted me to clear my thoughts of such seeming contradictions.

Off I went on a Bible search of the word "compassion." I quickly realized that there was a rich mosaic of God's person on display. It seemed for a bit that mercy and compassion were almost interchangeable. Not a God who had mercy on me when he could have crushed me, but rather a God sympathetic to the reality that I am but dust and clay—a cracked pot. God was the Father—the progenitor and source—of all mercy. The God of all comfort! He had been the God of all discomfort in my youth. Years later, pastors still enjoyed holding a frightening and intimidating God over my head and my life. These words that I read in Scripture were incessant testimony to the most beautiful person in the universe, indeed a person with infinite assets, the Father of lights, in whom there is no darkness or shadows of the crap I was taught in the past.

As I jumped around Scripture with joy, one word kept drawing my attention: primarily translated as "compassion," occasionally as "mercy" or "tender mercies," it transliterates as *splaggnon* in multiple forms. The word harks back to the time when internal organs were used to refer to our emotions. The heart pumps blood, but our heartfelt love comes from the center and depth of our person. In the translation of "compassion," *splaggno*n even takes on a gut-level experience.

As I sat there, I began to realize that Jesus had not only promised never to leave me or forsake me, but that he was experiencing my pain with me. He bore our griefs and sorrows on the cross, and he was bearing them again with me. For twenty years I had been told that the three persons of the Godhead indwelt me for various and sundry reasons, none of them very practical or noticeable at the time. Here Jesus was telling me that, not only was he with me, was experiencing my pain with me, was sharing my burden, was protecting me from destruction—but also that Holy Spirit was so engaged as to be making "requests of my Abba for me, with groanings too deep for words" (Romans 8:26). His words were much more effective than the little white pills I had been taking.

CHAPTER 26
I SEE THE STARS AND ROWLAND THUNDER

*You, Lord, in the beginning laid the foundations of the heavens
and the earth, and the heavens are the work of your hands.
They will perish but you remain; and they will all grow old
like a garment; like a cloak you will fold them up, and they
will be changed.*
—Hebrews 1: 10–12

*But the day of the Lord will come as a thief in the night, in
which the heavens will pass away with a great noise, and the
elements will melt with a fervent heat; both the earth and the
works in it shall be burnt up.*
—2 Peter 3:10

As I read Psalm 147, I felt the encouragement of the Lord in verse 3, where the psalmist speaks to our broken heart; but this time my eyes got caught on verse four: "He counts the number of the stars; he calls them all by name." My first encounter with the stars was a "bigger brother" experience. Rowland wasn't my "biggest brother," but being my second oldest brother, eight years older than me, he was also a lot bigger than me. By seventh grade he could palm a basketball. By the time he was fifteen, he stood a manly six-foot-three—not a skinny kid or an overweight teen—and he could easily pass as a man in a man's world.

My early relationship with Rowland reminded me of a scene Annie and I encountered one summer afternoon when we returned to our homestead. We kept a number of our young German shepherd males in temporary kennels under the shade of tall oaks along the creek side of our property. Set on concrete blocks for support, and filled with sand floors, the portable kennels allowed us many options. On this day they housed two brothers from different fathers: they were separated in age by about eighteen months, the four-month-old pup being maybe a third the size of his fully grown, teenage brother. They were also separated by a 6-foot by 6-foot wire fence, or so we thought.

When we glanced ahead toward their kennels as we drove on the yard, it looked like Cody, our four-month-old pup, was missing. We quickly parked our van and hopped out to get a closer look. Running toward their kennel, we stopped dead in our tracks, not knowing whether to laugh or panic. As we were training them to be competition dogs, we were never supposed to let them interact freely, because one dog should never have the opportunity to dominate the other. They were all trained to be the dominant dog, the winning dog—never submitting to another. Moreover, we had no idea how a fully grown teenager would treat his little brother. But there they sat, Cody now inside the kennel of his big brother, Augie, his back to his own kennel, staring at Augie, who was sitting about two feet away. While we were gone, they had dug about two feet under their common fence, and Cody had tunneled through into Augie's pen. We had no idea how long they had been together, but they now sat looking at each other as though they had run out of good ideas for fun.

147

Unlike Augie, my brother Rowland never ran out of ideas. On a cold winter afternoon when conditions were about perfect, he asked my sister Patricia and me if we wanted to join him for a sled ride down our long, slick, snow-covered driveway. With a nice slope, it made for an exhilarating and extensive ride. We got onto Rowland's sled—he on the bottom and me on top, Patricia in between, piled like a short stack of pancakes. Off we went, quickly gaining speed, when I saw Rowland whispering to Patricia. I soon discovered that I was not a pancake, but more like a sausage link that Rowland had ordered Pat to jettison. As I bounced across the snow, the two of them roared down the hill convulsed with laughter—that is, until Pat met a similar fate when Rowland tilted her off the other side of the sled. My spirits were immediately lifted to see that my sister had suffered the same fate as I had.

Fast-forward to yet another frigid winter evening. Reluctant to brave the sub-zero temperatures in order to care for my bevy of rabbits (my first attempt at free enter-prise), I lingered in our bedroom with some entertaining distraction. Just then Rowland stepped in and asked me if I had fed my rabbits. Upon hearing my negative reply, he asked me if I would like to trade my outdoor responsibil-ities for a thorough cleaning of our bedroom, for which he was responsible. Considering the weather, I figured it was a fair deal and agreed. As I began the boring chore of finding a proper place for all the things strewn around the room, Rowland hopped on the bed and cracked open a magazine. Leary of the possibility that he might welsh on his part of the bargain, I asked him when he was going to feed and water the rabbits, which would require defrosting all the water bowls. He smiled and, with maximum effect, informed me that Mother had told him to take care of my rabbits before he came inside—and that the chore was already done. What a con artist!

Duly aware of Rowland's ways, I became wary of any of his subsequent offers. We were roommates in a ground-floor bedroom, and Rowland came home one cool summer night and woke me from my sleep to ask if I wanted to see the Big Dipper. The only big dipper I was aware of was the one my mother used to scoop ice cream. At seven years old, I had absolutely no idea. He talked about the Little Dipper, the Big Dipper, and the Milky Way, and all I could think of was the candy bars we sold in our dairy store at the bottom of the hill. It's in the sky, he said. Let's climb out the window, and I'll show you! Everybody was asleep, and now he was trying to con me into going out the window. This was my last chance at any control. Once out the window, would he re-hook the screen, and leave me in the middle of our rural, creepy, boogey-man side yard, which would require me to circle the house in my bare feet to get in through our unlocked back door? What if I fell in our sewage ditch and had septic water up to my knees—for an ice cream scoop in the sky! No way.

He walked over to the window and unhooked the two eye hooks. Tilting the screen out, he raised it up off the two latches at the top and then set it outside the window. I didn't figure I had much choice, but I was going to make him go first, even though I knew he could dive back in and lock me out. Oh well, life takes courage.

Out we went, both scanning the sky—he looking for the Big Dipper, me for an ice cream scoop. There it is, he whispered, pointing in the direction he was looking. I looked and saw nothing. It wasn't until years later that I understood I was supposed to be looking for stars config-ured in the form of a ladle and that I wasn't looking for a soup ladle that had somehow ended up in the sky. Rowland and I gazed for a long time, unbothered by light pollution, time, or people. The night sky revealed a beauty that was still unforgettable some forty years later.

⟜ • ⟞

As I gained a little bit of emotional steam, I wondered whether I could ratchet up my schooling. What better way than to sign up for an astronomy course at the local junior college. Not only was it something I was interested in; it would fulfill my science elective requirement and leave me free of butchering any frogs. In a class filled with mostly teenagers, I had a blast. Professor Verba (everyone called him Vrb) was a retired high-school science teacher who was really engaging and invested in his subject. Both of us were in our fifties, and we developed a quick rapport.

In one class, Vrb was entertaining the likelihood of the big-bang theory. I interjected that the Bible would support that notion, quoting Proverbs 8:26: "While as yet He [God] had not made the earth or the fields, or the primal dust of the world." Kind of like Emeril Lagasse in the kitchen: God spoke and Bang, there was! Must have been a heck of a bang, Vrb. The class sat in silence, waiting for Vrb's retort; his brain was busy, but his tongue was idle as he considered that option.

Vrb would lecture about the stars, some dead, even though their light was still making it to earth. I would sit and read at home in the book of Isaiah or in Psalms, where God had been the first to name all the stars, call them all by name as he sustained them, never losing track of even one. Then, incredibly, one evening Vrb was speaking about the earth's ultimate demise. I told him that there was a passage—actually two, one in the Psalms and repeated in Hebrews 1—where Jesus folds up the heavens and the earth like a large outer garment, and they combust. Vrb responded that, from what we can tell, that's pretty much the way the story ends!

The semester was soon over, but the Lord had used the class to express his playfulness with regard to his awesome creation. I am hoping he will someday let me speak a star into existence, or at least let me stand by as he does. I will have to look out for Rowland, who might be trying to position me in front of the Lord, seeing if I might get an unexpected astronomical ride throughout the universe.

CHAPTER 27
I SHOULD HAVE
BEEN CRUCIFIED

Therefore, we were buried with him through baptism
into death.
—Romans 6:4

For he who has died has been freed from sin. Now if we
died with Christ, we believe that we shall also live with
him, knowing that Christ, having been raised from the dead,
dies no more.
—Romans 6:7–9

Nevertheless, when one turns to the Lord, the veil is taken
away. Now the Lord is the Spirit; and where the Spirit of the
Lord is, there is liberty.
—2 Corinthians 3:16–17

Throughout my life, no matter what the pain, I had learned to carry it. Whether it was lack of opportunity, rejection, failure, disappointing success, misplaced optimism, or a list of sins that might include shame, guilt, anxiety, worry, or fear of failure—I had taken it all and stuffed it anywhere I could find room, and had covered it with enough biblical rationale so that, I hoped, it wouldn't rear its ugliness in my life again. But for the last two and a half years, God had no longer let me live with my pain. He immersed me in it. In his infinite wisdom he had hedged me in: I was locked up, the lights were out, and he was the key. There had been no way out. I had a better chance of escaping from the depths of an abandoned mineshaft. All the while, I kept my nose to the ground, tracking for God like a police dog sniffing for the bad guy. God played hide-and-seek with me until all I looked for was him; and he hid from me until all I wanted was him.

Pain may be one of life's best-kept secrets: it certainly isn't something we want to hear about. If we did, therapists wouldn't get hundreds of dollars an hour to listen. Nor do we want to talk about it, or those same therapists wouldn't have to extract it from us with the biggest pliers in their toolbox. But it turns out that pain is paradoxically the key to life's success. Until we are so overwhelmed, we have no chance for true success. The only pain that can make us alive again is the pain that killed us in the first place. Only the pain we can't carry is the pain that can change us. The paradox of the Christian message is that we must die before we can live.

If we are honest with ourselves, I think we all want a prosperity gospel. At some level, we want a life of abundance. The testimony of the Bible suggests that we were created for blessing, and God is in the blessing business. The problem is that we and God have different ideas of what that looks like. We want a life free of stress, free of cares. We want a life of good health, lots of people who love us, and always a life of more—more than we have, more than we need, even more than we want. And there are days, depending on how we read our Bibles, when we have good reason to think that this is what God wants for us, too. We often develop a "be good and God will bless you" motif from the Bible.

Early Christian life experiences would often seem to reinforce these notions. Depending on one's previous life, good behavior can be its own reward. Generally speaking, the new life in Jesus is an exciting and stimulating change. Others might leave the impression that accepting Jesus is the end of a person's problems. But there are parallel realities. The Bible speaks of our *positional* reality and our *experiential* reality. When we trust in Jesus, all the things God has done for us become ours. We don't experience them at that moment; but it is who we are in Christ—our position in him—reality as God has declared it.

Pastors frequently see only the attractive truths. They admonish their parishioners to claim their new status in Christ. They might even distort spiritual riches in Christ into a prosperity gospel. What they often forget is that we have a God of genius who declares, "Blessed are the poor in spirit" and "Blessed are you who mourn." Yet we remain too blind and deaf to comprehend.

Consider for a moment the church's sacrament of believer's baptism. Here the new believer goes under the water to portray death with Jesus (positionally) and is then lifted up to signify the resurrected life with him. These ceremonies are usually filled with joy and celebration—and rightfully so. A soul delivered from depths of self to life in Jesus. But maybe, when a candidate is baptized, the baptizer should hold him under until he feels like he has been waterboarded. As he is raised to newness of life, he breaks out of the water spitting and hollering, "Jesus, you about drowned me." And a voice from heaven answers, "Yes, my dear brother, but I had to."

Prior to these two and a half years, I would have never imagined that I had to be crucified. Little did I know that I would get that very opportunity. Over the course of my life, I have sat in myriad churches, Christian groups with a variety of persuasions and distinctives. I have read hundreds, if not thousands, of books by Christian authors on countless aspects of the Christian life. I never read anything that spoke to the pain I was experiencing until I picked up a book I had not seen by an author I had enjoyed and respected for almost thirty years. In fact, I remembered my lament from years earlier that more of his work was not published and available. In my opinion, A. W. Tozer is one of the more fascinating and practical Christian thinkers who has ever come to light. Though a modern evangelical through and through, his walk with Jesus left him comfortable even in the realm of Christian mysticism. Such a hybrid thinker found the words to express the believer's crucifixion in very understandable terms. In his short classic *The Pursuit of God*, Tozer speaks of the rending of the veil that stands between us and our view of God. He attributes this veil to the "self-sins." Before he directly addresses the solution, he talks of the subtleties and strength of the self.

> One should suppose that proper instruction in the doctrines of man's depravity and the necessity for justification through the righteousness of Christ alone would deliver us from the power of the self-sins, but it does not work that way. Self can live unrebuked at the very altar. It can watch the bleeding Victim [Jesus] die and not be in the least affected by what it sees. It can fight for the faith of the reformers and preach eloquently the creed of salvation by grace and gain

strength by its efforts. To tell the truth, it seems actually to feed upon orthodoxy and is more at home in a Bible conference than in a tavern. Our very state of longing after God may afford it an excellent condition under which to thrive and grow. (A.W. Tozer, *Pursuit of God* [Camp Hill, PA: Christian Publications, 1982, 1993])

Next comes the scary part, the part you wouldn't wish on your worst enemy, and yet hope the Lord brings to every friend. And for me, it was the part that finally made sense of the past two and half years of my life.

Self is the opaque veil that hides the face of God from us. It can be removed only in spiritual experience, never by mere instruction. We may as well try to instruct leprosy out of our system. There must be a work of God in destruction before we are free. We must invite the cross to do its deadly work within us. We must bring our self-sins to the cross for judgment. We must prepare ourselves for an ordeal of suffering in some measure like that through which our Savior passed when He suffered under Pontius Pilate.

Let us remember that when we talk of the rending of the veil, we are speaking in a figure, and the thought of it is poetical, almost pleasant, but in actuality there is nothing pleasant about it. In human experience that veil is made of living spiritual tissue; it is composed of the sentient, quivering stuff of which our whole beings consist, and to touch it is to touch us where we feel pain. To tear it away is to injure us, to hurt us and make us bleed. To say otherwise is to make the cross, no cross and to make death, no death at all. It is never fun to die. To rip through the dear and tender stuff of which life is made can never be anything but deeply painful. Yet that is what the cross did to Jesus, and it is what the cross would do to every man to set him free. (pp. 43-45)

Tozer then lets his reader know that this is not some do-it-yourself solution:

Let us beware of tinkering with our inner life, hoping ourselves to rend the veil. God must do everything for us. Our part is to yield and trust. We must confess, forsake, repudiate the self-life, and then reckon it crucified. But we must be careful to distinguish lazy "acceptance" from the real work of God. We must insist upon the work being done. We dare not rest content with a neat doctrine of self-crucifixion. That is to imitate Saul and spare the best of the sheep and the oxen.

Insist that the work be done in very truth and it will be done. The cross is rough and it is deadly, but it is effective. It does not keep its victim hanging there forever. There comes a moment when its work is finished and the suffering victim dies. After that is resurrection glory and power, and the pain is forgotten for joy that the veil is taken away and we have

entered in actual spiritual experience the presence of the living God. (pp 43-45)

In this short narrative by Tozer, God had put the frosting
on the cake of my understanding. God had kept me in the
dark for all this time, grasping for comfort, and instead he
allowed me to catch him. Now, as he had become mine, he
continued to loosen the chains of darkness and despair with
his explanation of what had transpired in my life.

CHAPTER 28
SEE ME, FEEL ME, TOUCH ME, HEAL ME

Suddenly a hand touched me—And he said to me, "O Daniel, man greatly beloved, understand the words I speak to you—." Then he said to me, "Daniel from the first day you set your heart to understand, and to humble yourself before your God, your words were heard and I have come because of your words."
—Daniel 10:10–12

Then again, the one having the likeness of a man touched me and strengthened me. And he said, "O man greatly beloved, fear not! Peace be to you; be strong, yes, be strong!"
—Daniel 10:18

But Jesus said, "Somebody touched me, for I perceived power going out from me."
—Luke 8:46

But Jesus answered and said, "Permit even this." And he touched his ear and healed him.
—Luke 22:51

I continued to scoot along at a nice clip at school. I had matriculated nonstop for twenty-one months. My communications curriculum was finished, and I was knocking off electives two at a time. It was now summer, and I could see that by fall I would be down to a Greek course that I wanted to take for both undergraduate and graduate credit; a couple of theology courses I could take by correspondence; and one or two more five-week courses to polish off my degree requirements. It was time to turn my energy toward the prospect of employment.

With plans to go on to graduate school, coupled with overwhelming apprehension at the thought of going back to work, I looked for something part-time that I could do in the evening. I did not fear work, which had always been my preferred form of recreation; instead, it was the fear that I would be overcome emotionally in any kind of socially demanding environment. I was born an introvert: when Adam went off to hide from God in the Garden of Eden, he was carrying me in his loins. Coupling that introversion with social insularity (other than the members of my family) until I was sent off to Sunday school with the threat of a spanking if I cried, I was behind the social curve right from the get-go.

My parents were committed to Christian education but were too poor to afford us the luxury of kindergarten, which left me isolated when I began first grade. My mother had prepared me academically for a third-grade curriculum, but socially, I would have struggled even at a preschool level. Then, nearing the age of nine, when I broke my arm and lay in traction for a month, I was surprised by how stressful it was just to return to Sunday school. Vulnerable, with my injury still healing, I sat there as the superintendent led the kids in the song "Just as I Am, Without One Plea." An unattractive tune to me when I was healthy, it left me emotionally flummoxed and physically on the edge of vomiting.

Now, as I contemplated thoughts of employment, that same set of feelings combined with what had become a significantly adverse day. Emotions were running rampant, creating the perfect storm. Suddenly, I felt like I was back to square one, as distressed as I had been almost three years before. Overwhelmed by the seeming loss of ground, feeling that I could take no more, I was ready to throw in the towel. And then I did something no one ever gave me permission to do.

I was raised in an environment of religious prohibition, where it was easier to live a life of don'ts than one of do's. This had made for an easy transition into doctrinal fundamentalism at twenty. Neither environment had allowed for outside-the-box thinking or behavior. Typically, if you weren't given specific permission to think or say something, it was healthy to assume that it was unacceptable. I was already nearing forty when I heard Charles Stanley cite his freedom to speak to Jesus. The religious formalism of my experience never allowed for the free and easy exchange that we felt the disciples and others had with Jesus. It was a real head-scratcher for me to see these biblical citations of day-to-day interactions, and then to be told that all our prayers had to be addressed to the Father, notwithstanding the notion I had of just wanting to talk in a less than prayerful state of mind.

I had already been set free to a great extent, and prayer was no longer a formality, a ritual groveling, or some kind of pious exercise. It had become a conversation with fellow family members. But on this day, I was in too much pain to think, and all that came out of my mouth was an excruciating "Jesus, Jesus, Jesus!" As I tried to formulate some thought to express, I suddenly felt a surge of warmth and peace radiate throughout my body from my shoulder down to my waist. Someone was touching me! About two and a half feet from my desk to my left and about three feet inside my study door, I could sense the presence of someone standing. I sat in stunned silence. Suddenly my emotions were calm. As I looked closer, the invisible presence remained. Then, after a brief moment, the presence faded away. I don't know who was there, but I know who I had been talking to. I wouldn't want to bet my eternal birthright on it, but I'm thinking it was Jesus. I was thankful that I didn't need anyone's permission before it could happen, and I'm thankful that I now need no one's authorization to acknowledge that it did.

That experience changed my life. It happened at such a juncture in God's healing process of my soul that I was able to totally accept and absorb it. In my mind it was an intimate, personal visit from the Brother who loves me, totally expressing his love for me and coming alongside me with the ultimate comfort. The timing leapfrogged my recovery to the point where I had the solid footing to go forward with the secret knowledge that everything was going to be okay. Though I could still see some big hurdles before me, mountains in the distance, I had a new confidence that I was going to survive, that this seeming dark night of the soul was eventually going to end now, after almost three years — sooner rather than later.

⊃ • ⊂

As I perused the classifieds, I looked for something as nonsocial as possible. I knew that getting around people would be healthy and the next step in my recovery, but I didn't think that I could take a very big dose to start with. Humanity's innate curiosity can make us nosy even without an agenda. The last thing I wanted was to have anyone get a glimpse of my pain. In front of God it was okay to be naked, but I still wanted to be fully dressed when I was with other people. As I looked through the classifieds, my eyes fell on a truck-driving job. I thought this could be the answer. I was capable of driving eighteen-wheelers and anything smaller. When I saw that the very newspaper I was reading was looking for part-time night drivers for their heavy-duty commercial trucks, I was thrilled. The listing suggested that there would be some truck loading involved, which would give me some exercise, but for most of the time I figured I would be by myself, behind the wheel, in the dark of night. Perfect!

Well, not so perfect. God had tricked me again. I walked in on Labor Day evening, full of nerves—exactly three years from the day I had left my home and Annie—punched in, and proceeded to the dock area. I soon learned that little time would be spent driving. Instead, I would be stacking and wrapping newspaper inserts, then loading trucks. I headed for an assignment, choosing the stacking platform at one end zone of the large staging area, the farthest spot from the rest of human activity. The emotional battle raged. Four to six other men—of varying cultural distinctions— and I waited on each side of a conveyor belt that spit out five- to fifty-pound bales of papers to be stacked on pallets. The social climate was dark, and the work was drudgery, with no hope in sight. What had I done?!

Work had always been my go-to activity in life. I was usually quick to catch on and was soon leading the way. But my new situation made shoveling coal in hell look attractive. Failure or quitting, however, were not options. I needed to reorient to a normal life, if at all possible. I dug in. I started praying for everybody and everything! One can only imagine how big God's plans are. I was just trying to do my part in responding to his healing of me, "the working out of my own salvation" response to the provision and call of God. I found that my deliverance included the men I worked with: Indians with doctorates, Pakistanis with pedigrees, soft-spoken Hispanics, one Spanish-speaking Albanian, jive-talking blacks, and white guys with more opinions than thoughts. God had me praying for us all!

I started to relax. As the new guy, I carried my own weight and more. My demeanor brightened as I realized that I was going to survive my reintroduction into the work world. I saw my way through the noise and chaos, and I realized that I was on the backside of another mountain. This was going to be a piece of cake!

CHAPTER 29
EPITAPH FOR A MARRIAGE

For our God is a consuming fire.
—Hebrews 12:29

I in them and you in me; that they may be made perfect in one,
and the world may know that you have sent me and have
loved them as you have loved me.
—John 17:23

Love suffers long, does not seek its own, does not rejoice in
iniquity, bears all things, believes all things, hopes all things,
endures all things.
—1 Corinthians 13:4–6

December roared into Chicago snowing and blowing. As the city came to a crawl, my life continued on the upswing. The finish line for my undergraduate degree was straight ahead. I had camaraderie with my fellow workers, the respect of my supervisors, and the job was a good physical workout. My life was taking on a normality for the first time in more than three years—as my pain was disappearing.

Christmas fast approached as I eagerly anticipated dinner with my friends Dave and Kathy. Dave and I were good friends, though the dynamics of our lives had separated us geographically and responsibilities had filled our time. Nonetheless, Dave had engaged with me over the last three years in my "Howdy Partners" email group. In those interchanges, some folks read my emails and kept their thoughts to themselves. Some even blocked the messages because of their mind-altering content. Dave, on the other hand, engaged with me and often responded in a way that was reminiscent of our great times after church those years before. The soul synergy created by mutual engagement in the things of God had been a source of great blessing in my time of travail. And now, having dinner with Dave and Kathy would mark my first true social outing without my soul crutches. I was still walking gingerly, but I was walking.

My mood was almost festive. Just three years earlier, there had been little hope that I could ever listen to Bing Crosby or Johnny Mathis again. "White Christmas," for example, tore my heart out, when I knew that the rest of my Christmases would be black. Now the joy was back at table with my friends. I enjoyed the break from school and work, and Dave and Kathy were fresh from the holiday sights of downtown Chicago. As we sat in a suburban eatery, lingering over dessert after an exquisite meal, the conversation turned to central Indiana for a moment. Though I grew up just thirty miles from downtown Chicago, my soul much preferred the expansiveness of the heartland, where there were more deer than people. As my thoughts slipped back to my beloved hobby farm, my mind got caught on Annie.

I made some weak comment theorizing that, as long as Annie didn't remarry, there was still hope for reconciliation in the plan of God. Kathy looked at Dave, and he nodded. I knew exactly what was coming. Calmly and gently, Kathy said she had seen Annie in a grocery store earlier in the month, and Annie was wearing a wedding ring. Kathy greeted Annie and soon got the news of her nuptials. I looked at Dave as I tried to maintain my composure. There were condolences on both their faces. I was distressed but not forlorn.

A complex of emotions met me when I returned home to my study. In my mind, Annie's marriage meant that we were irrevocably finished. That was the way I read my Bible—period, case closed. In acknowledging the finality of our marriage, I was reminded of what a pathetic husband I had been and that Annie certainly deserved better. I realized that, if I had wanted any chance at a successful marriage, I should have married at ten. At ten, when I met my new neighbor, Nancy, my biggest influence regarding the opposite sex had been my older sisters. Ranging in age from ten to fifteen years older than me, they were impressive by my standards. Full of life and always with cutting-edge thoughts and humor, they gave me a high regard for women and girls. My upbringing taught me to treat girls with kindness. Playing house with Nancy and her two younger sisters was free and easy, with a mutual appreciation for one another that allowed us to function as equals in our make-believe world of husband and wife.

Marriage in the cult made wives the biggest target of a legalistic religion's dogmatic disregard for the soul. Here, as is always the case, people were objectified in order to worship a god that's the creation of a petty authority. All the beauty of marriage, mutual love, and mutual submissiveness depicted in the Bible had been defoliated by a right-wing militant church trying to regain the ground lost in the culture wars of the 1960s and '70s. There I was, married and in charge of a piece of chattel property who supposedly was not smart enough to balance a checkbook, instead of in a relationship with the love of my life.

God's covenant between the three of us hadn't died easily. In fact, in his genius he had used my heart's desire, coupled with my heighted sense of responsibility, to totally transform my life. I had expressly asked to know what love is, to experience the love of God inside. Most of us would expect to experience God's love for us. That's not the way it worked. Instead of some warm, fuzzy, gentle, all lovey-dovey feeling with God, I experienced the love of God for Annie as he anguished and loved her to the end of our covenant. Because I didn't bail out on my love for Annie, in the end I had a ringside seat as Jesus loved her for four years of tribulation, until he covenanted with her in her new marriage.

And the payoff for me? I was caught up in the dynamic of God's love, a powerful storm, an all-consuming fire of passion for our marriage, for our souls, for our bond with him—because God is love, and his love will do whatever it takes. The fierceness of God's love, the infinitude of his commitment to anyone who has ever walked the earth, is beyond comprehension. We can only experience it, but we can never wrap our minds around it. And experience it I had!

But now I rested, assured that Annie was free of me and my mistakes. She had made her decisions—she had divorced and remarried—and she had her own life. And soon… so did I. In the next few months, the freedom of my circumstances and the soul the Lord had built within me came to the fore. I felt like that seventeen-year-old college student again, looking for his unicorn, this time with a soul full of life and love.

CHAPTER 30
ON TOP OF THE WORLD

"Look!" he answered, "I see four men loose, walking in the
midst of the fire; and they are not hurt, and the form of the
fourth is like the Son of God."
—Daniel 3:25

Then Jesus, being filled with the Holy Spirit, returned from
the Jordan and was led by the Spirit into the wilderness, being
tempted for forty days by the devil.
—Luke 4:1–2

Therefore, if anyone is in Christ, he is a new creation; the old
things have passed away; behold, all things have become new.
2 Corinthians 5:17

And this is eternal life, that they may know [experience] you,
the only true God and Jesus Christ whom you have sent.
—John 17:3

N ew Year's Day came and went, the days starting their
yawning stretch. Then, in a New York minute, winter
fled Chicago as if it had a tornado chasing its backside. All
the while, I had lassoed in the rest of my academic requirements, had become an acting supervisor at work, and was
prepared to walk the walk on graduation day. Friends and
family gathered from surrounding cities and states to party

with me on the big day. Jerry B. Jenkins was our commencement speaker, and he rescued what are typically boring proceedings with his sense of humor. A backflip by one young graduate and a somersault by another, while they received their newly minted diplomas, gave the proceedings a lively flavor. And me—there I was, thirty years late, and right on time!

The academics had a purpose, and my diploma might have some value, but the coup de grâce administered by the Lord had been my real *education*. Now, with less of me and more of Christ living in me, it had truly been a revelation.

The party soon ended, and I headed back home to my study. There I gave thanks to the God who had shown himself to me. I sat in awe and wonder as I thought about the God who put me at the top of the world. A God just aching to show himself to us. When we get close, our sins are going to ignite. Jesus will stand in the fire with us, and we will feel the burn, but we will be changed. This is the God Adam ran from. This is the God who, should he beckon us into his presence in our sinful state, the sight of his beauty would cause us to die of our guilt and shame. This is the God who wants the all of us. He will ask the impossible, and he'll let us die—for we (and our self-will) are the sacrifice—and then he will give us new life.

This "totally awesome" thing is not some teenage cliché. No, this is a shaking-in-your-boots, peeing-in-your pants, knee-buckling God. Not some Sunday morning Disney World God. Rather, he is the B-52 bomber that paints it on the numbers as he lands on the runway just inches from your body—where he has asked you to lie down. This is the totally he-she God, for God is both infinite masculinity and infinite femininity. She will comfort us. She will cover us with her wings. She will die in the fire to save us.

But he is the God who calls us to share in the sufferings of Jesus. He, even the Comforter, led Jesus out to the desert to be tempted by Satan for forty days. He will have nothing less than that we be conformed to the image of his unique Son, Jesus, the one who declared that he and the Father are one. This is the God who brought forth the perfect humanity of Jesus in order to have him absorb all the damning trash of our lives and experience in his perfect body all the stupid, shameful, disgusting, arrogant, truculent crap we ever produced—even our own filthy righteousness, rejected by God and thrown into the deepest sea. An omniscient God, choosing to forget every sin we ever committed, and thereby positing the one question that will stand for all eternity: "What think you of my beloved Son, Jesus Christ, the only one possessing the power to deliver you from your broken, mortal, troublesome, fading existence?" That is the first and last question, and there is only one good answer. We must change our minds from thinking that we are the center of the universe to acknowledging Jesus Christ as the person on whom the universe pivots, truly the firstborn among all creation. And then we are in for a ride.

Pain may not be a language we at first understand, but it is a language that commands our attention. Pain is the language of a God who loves us. Pain gives us the humility to acknowledge who we are. Pain causes us to look outside ourselves, lest we die. We find God there—willing to be with us and in us—in our pain.

I guess I should have read my Bible a little more closely than I did. I never thought that God would let one of his children suffer like this. But I suspect I could have read it a million times and still missed it. There, all along, were God's purposes written by Job, possibly the oldest story in the Bible. In Job 42:5, Job says: "I have heard of you by

171

the hearing of the ear, but now my eyes [soul perception] see [experience] you." My prayer had been, "Whatever it takes, Lord, I want to know [experience] you. I want to know [experience] what love is, and I want you to show me!" It was a magnificent blunder!

EPILOGUE
FOREVER AND EVER, AMEN

Now the Lord blessed the latter days of Job more than his beginning.
—Job 42:12.

The crux of this story began with my pleading with the Lord, singing Foreigner's "I Want to Know What Love Is." It makes sense to conclude with "I Been Waiting for a Girl Like You."

Autumn leaves were falling when I returned from a long night of work. I lit up my computer to play some online bridge. When I located my desired website, up popped an ad for eHarmony. The matchmaking enterprise was promoting a six-month special, but what especially caught my eye was the personality test they offered. It would be an extensive questionnaire that promised a snapshot of my person. I liked personality tests, and since they promised almost immediate feedback, I engaged in what turned out to be a forty-five-minute exercise. When the results came back, I was surprised—pleasantly so! Their snapshot of me was spot-on. So I speculated: If they can develop an equally clear picture of a woman, there could be real merit to their offer. But I hesitated—after all, "real men don't eat quiche," and they don't date online either, do they? I suddenly realized that the clock had struck midnight, and the calendar had turned to my birthday. I reached in my wallet for my charge card and, as I sang "Happy Birthday" to myself, signed up for six months of online opportunities.

This turned out to be quite the investment, and later I laughed about my hesitance. Here were more women than I knew what to do with, and they all were expressing proper motivation. There wasn't all the mandatory game-playing that accompanies a lot of traditional dating circumstances. The women made clear their intentions, and eHarmony did their best to match those with similar profiles. Additionally, my Dutch frugality was pleased when I realized that I wouldn't have to waste $60 or more on a night that I would know, after five minutes, was going nowhere. This turned out to be a great way to presort the likelihood of any real interest and compatibility. Like any other situation in life, it required that the participant heed the well-known advice *caveat emptor* ("let the buyer beware"). One woman with whom I accepted a match reacted negatively when I told her that three of my male friends and I would play bridge at a Friday night church league, and then would retire to a small bar across the street to eat popcorn, drink beer, and solve all the world's problems. She said she found it interesting that I played bridge but surprising that I would join friends at a bar. I was now in my fifties, and I knew I didn't have the time or desire to explain to a woman of equal maturity that the first miracle my Savior performed was turning water into the best wine available in Israel at that moment in order to keep a wedding party going. I immediately halted that match.

Then, about six weeks in, eHarmony offered a match with a Michele from Milwaukee. Although I was living in the northwest suburbs of Chicago, Milwaukee was well within range. I accepted the match and she did likewise. As eHarmony managed our communications, I snuck in a

"Happy Thanksgiving" at the end of one of the lines desig-nated for a standard response to one of their standard ques-tions. Michele responded similarly, and I had my first hint that she, too, could live outside the box. We went through the website's standard protocols, which did not allow us to know anything more than each other's first names and locations. After a preliminary amount of communication, they gave us the option to release our photo to the corre-sponding party. Up to that moment we had engaged in some substantial e-conversations; now neither one of us wanted to waste time. Michele released her photo, saying that I should decide whether I thought there would be any chem-istry between us. Considering the weighty nature of some of our website "conversations," coupled with her photo, I thought that not only would there be chemistry; a strong likelihood existed that there might be some physics as well.

As our conversations evolved, they were both in-depth and mundane. I remember inquiring whether there were some cafes near Lake Michigan and near where she lived or worked—since I was considering possible places for a rendezvous. She suggested that there were, and I looked forward to the possibilities. As I focused on her picture, something caught my attention. She had said that she and her sister owned a shop. She wouldn't tell me what kind of shop or where it was located—along with a protective silence about other vitals—in order to guarantee her ano-nymity. But she did say that her sister had taken the photo she had sent me at their store. As I looked more closely at the photo, I told Michele that I thought I knew what kind of store they operated. Behind her in the photograph was a shelf with what looked like white-topped bottles. I told her that it seemed to me they must own a "Lotions and Potions" type of shop. Her reply: "No, guess again." Game on! I was disappointed in my failure, but glad for her playful response, and I didn't plan on being wrong twice. This was going to require some effort.

Then one day, as I meandered through the aisles at Walmart looking for a new shower liner, I walked past what looked like bolts of fabric. The white of the bolt stuck out on each end of the fabric, and it struck me that that had to be what was behind Michele in her photo. I found my shower liner and quickly went home to my computer, where I jumped on the internet and inquired about fabric stores in Milwaukee. It came up with a list, which I quickly narrowed down by eliminating any national chain-type stores. This left a handful of independent shops to choose from. I speculated about what her sister might have named their shop and headed for that website. As I scanned the location, I saw some lakeside photos of employees and customers in different situations. I couldn't get a close-up on the photos to help me determine whether Michele appeared in any of them, but I had a good feeling that I was getting warmer. I Googled this shop's location and discovered that it was just a few blocks off Lake Michigan. I checked out the other shops, and none of them were near the lake. This had to be it.

At that point we were still required to use eHarmony's website to communicate, and the only thing we knew for sure was each other's first names. By this time I was highly interested in Michele, and yet I didn't want to scare her off. In my next message to her, I began by explaining just that; then I gave her my full name, address, and telephone number, so that she could feel as fully informed as I was. I proceeded to tell her that I was quite sure that she and her sister owned The Cutting Table, at 2499 S. Delaware Ave. in Milwaukee, and that their phone number was (414)

555-3747. Michele was quick to respond, and her reply began with the salutation "Dear Sherlock." As I sat laughing, I began singing "I Been Waiting for a Girl Like You" as a wave of euphoria came over me. I keyed up a U-tube video of the song and sang along in full throat. This was icing on the cake. Matched in November, we met in January, and we married in May. So far, it has been a thirteen-year party — with all the vagaries of life thrown in. And let the record state that, in all of my attendant circumstances, the Lord is blessing my latter days more than the beginning. As I sign off, I invite readers to embrace their pain and allow it to become a journey toward awe and wonder.

ACKNOWLEDGMENTS

Whereas God knew the end before the beginning and surely remained at ease, it appeared to me that my end was to arrive shortly after the beginning—leaving me dis-eased. It is with immense gratitude that I would like to acknowledge those whom the Lord was able to use to facilitate his intended outcome.

Like the iconic roll of Lifesavers, my life-savers came in assorted varieties: my wise and caring counselors, Shawn Pogue and Cal Elifson, who nurtured the life that was within me, drawing me through God's love for me; my former sister-in-law Carol Stewart, whose reassuring letter of acceptance (should my marriage survive) arrived at a dark and dismal moment; my friends Dave Church and Lynn Alderin, as different as night and day, but both available in many a critical moment in their own *assigned* way; even the encouraging words of Walt Wangerin Jr. in a momentary encounter, expressing his wisdom concerning my circumstances. Most importantly, I want to acknowledge my sisters Patricia and Elaine, whose care for me was unconditional, as they entered into my pain and stood in the fire with me.

With regard to the writing and production of this book, there is another band of brothers, though they, too, are mostly women. First and foremost, my dear and loving wife, Michele, who for thirteen years now has been my best friend and greatest encouragement. She embodies the virtuous wife of Proverbs 30:10-31, and for that I thank both her and the Lord. My sister Lori's encouraging words aided in checking my memory about things having to do with our family and its history. I also note her referring me to my editor, the namesake of our venerable grandpa, Reinder Van Til, who slogged through my novice ways and kept me pointed toward my true north. And finally, to you, the reader, thank you for sticking with me to the end. It is my hope that the Lord will use my story and his love to draw you closer to him.